S0-AYF-087

.B88
1985

Better Spelling

Fourteen Steps to Spelling Improvement

THIRD EDITION

James I. Brown

Thomas E. Pearsall
University of Minnesota

D. C. HEATH AND COMPANY

Lexington, Massachusetts   Toronto

KALAMAZOO VALLEY
COMMUNITY COLLEGE
LIBRARY

Copyright © 1985 by D. C. Heath and Company.
Previous editions copyright © 1971 and 1978 by D. C. Heath and Company.

All rights reserved. No part of this publication may be reproduced or transmitted in any form or by any means, electronic or mechanical, including photocopy, recording, or any information storage or retrieval system, without permission in writing from the publisher.

Published simultaneously in Canada.

Printed in the United States of America.

International Standard Book Number: 0-669-07653-8

Contents

Introduction   vii
Diagnosis   1

Part One   **Auditory-Centered Problems**

1   Words with *ie, ei*   19
2   Final *y*   23
3   The Final Consonant Rule   29
4   Vowel Length   35
5   Pronunciation Difficulties   39
6   Unstressed Vowels   45
7   Sound-Alikes   51

Part Two   **Visual-Centered Problems**

8   Additive Elements   63
9   Final *e*   67
10   Assimilative Changes   73
11   Plurals   83
12   The Hyphen   93
13   Apostrophes   99
14   The Demons   111
15   Using Your Dictionary   113

     Progress Check   116

     A Final Word   123

     Appendix
       Core Words   125
       Supplementary List   129
       State Abbreviations and Metric Terms   131
       Personal Spelling List   132

Introduction

So you want to do something about your spelling? You want to make it an asset, not a liability? How to succeed in business, in school, or in life without spelling well does pose a problem.

A recent survey was made of personnel officers in the 500 largest corporations in the United States to determine preferences in job application letters and personal resumes. Of the fifty-one items under consideration, "Good grammar and spelling are essential in a letter of application" was rated above all other considerations.*

Did you ever stop to think that a single misspelling can keep you from getting a job — or being promoted? It can indeed. Spelling happens to be one of the few fixed and certain things about our language. Furthermore, a spelling error is always down in black and white for everyone to see. Many consider misspellings as clear evidence of lack of education, lack of intelligence, or carelessness. If you don't like that impression, work on spelling. Put your best spelling forward. It pays.

This book is designed to help you solve your spelling problem, to provide maximum help in minimum space. In short, this is a little book for a big problem. The emphasis is on five key principles.

1. *Meeting common needs:* In one study not a single college graduate could spell all of the following twenty words correctly: *bragadocio, accomodate, rarafy, liquafy, pavillion, vermillion, imposter, moccassin, asinnine, concensus, rococoe, titilate, sacriligious, mayonaise, impreserio, innoculate, supercede, oblagato, dessicate, resussitate.* Since all 20 words are misspelled, see how many you can spell correctly. Spelling even 12 right puts you in a class by yourself. Only one in 10 managed that. Answers are on page ix.

Now take another look at that list. According to Thorndike's research, two of those words are so uncommon that they didn't appear even once in a random count of 18 million written words. And only half of the words

* See *The ABCA Bulletin,* June, 1981, pp. 3–7.

appeared one or more times in a million words. After all, how often do you write *obligato* or *desiccate*?

In this text, the emphasis is on words you use *every* day, not every three years. You don't need to swallow a dictionary. Just be sure to use it on those occasions when you need to spell such infrequently used words.

Furthermore, we've selected from the words most frequently written, those that pose particular spelling problems. They make up what might be called the crucial core. Once you learn how to spell them, you eliminate about 90 percent of your spelling difficulties. To arrive at such a core, we have consolidated nine different lists of commonly misspelled words. The resulting list of 336 words, found on page 125, contains those words that appeared on three or more of the original lists. Using this list of core words, you can concentrate on those most deserving attention. You'll also find a supplementary list of 235 slightly less troublesome words.

2. *Learning much through little:* You can learn to spell the long way — one word at a time — and learn, for example, to spell 600 words containing *ei* or *ie*. Or you can learn a single rule that will enable you to spell all 600 immediately, save for the few inevitable exceptions, which you can always learn separately.

This text takes you along the shorter route, providing you with 14 principles to speed your progress. Thus, in learning to spell the relatively few core words, you are actually learning to spell thousands of related words.

3. *Using programmed instruction:* The greater your active involvement, the better your results. For that reason, portions of this book are in programmed form, sometimes of the more customary sort, sometimes of a new specially devised self-discovery type. Both types demand active written responses on your part, to ensure more rapid mastery.

4. *Isolating problem areas:* Since your problem areas in spelling may be many or few, the sooner you can identify them accurately, the sooner you can solve them. That's why the book begins with diagnosis. The diagnostic test you will take is perhaps the most complete test yet devised. It will isolate 14 separate problem areas and let you compare your proofreading performance with your spelling performance, an additional insight of importance.

Finally, you should know whether your spelling problems rise more from what you see or from what you hear. When you spell, what *do* you rely on most — the way the word looks or the way it sounds? Compare your scores on the two parts of the diagnostic test. See if you are predominantly eye-minded or ear-minded. That's worth knowing if you're to progress as rapidly as you should.

5. *Personalizing the approach:* While every effort has been made to tailor this book to your individual needs, you can take two additional steps yourself to carry on the effort. At the end of the book be sure to take advantage of the space where you're to list any and every word you find yourself misspelling. This self-made list is, of course, more valuable than any list made by others for it reflects the very words *you* yourself have trouble with. These are your spelling demons.

Next, make full use of the two lists at the end of the book. From time to time, have someone read you 20 words from a list, putting each into an appropriate sentence context. Try to spell the words, putting a check by any that still give you trouble until you gradually master both lists.

Accelerating gains through TV: To provide additional help in the mastery of this text, nine closely integrated spelling videotapes have been developed. After all, spelling is essentially a visual activity. TV, with its ability to create dramatic images, provides an ideal medium for supplementing the written word and speeding the learning process. As the Chinese proverb goes, "One picture is worth more than a thousand words." When you combine TV pictures with words from this text, you have an especially effective combination. The nine tapes provide that important visual facet, focusing on the diagnosis of individual problems and needs, on ways of using the self-interpreting profile, on special visualizing techniques, and on ways of capitalizing on mnemonic, visual, auditory, and kinesthetic devices.

To our knowledge, this is the only spelling book yet written that has such closely coordinated videotapes for closed-circuit use in learning labs or learning resource centers. Initial research published in *Toward Better Teaching** revealed that the tapes improved the average student's performance from 76 percent accuracy to 93 percent accuracy. For students with more serious spelling problems, gains were even greater — 40 percent improvement.

The tapes are available from a nonprofit organization: Telstar Productions, Inc., 366 North Prior, St. Paul, Minnesota 55104.

Answers: braggadocio, accommodate, rarefy, liquefy, pavilion, vermilion, impostor, moccasin, asinine, consensus, rococo, titillate, sacrilegious, mayonnaise, impresario, inoculate, supersede, obligato, desiccate, resuscitate

---

* "To Develop or Not to Develop," by James I. Brown and Lyman K. Steil, *Toward Better Teaching,* University of Minnesota, Vol. 6, No. 3 (May 1973), pp. 1–2.

Diagnosis

Your first step, as the Greeks put it, is to "know thyself." After all, you can hardly eliminate your spelling difficulties if you don't know exactly what they are. That's why you should begin by taking the diagnostic test that follows.

It will pinpoint 14 potential problem areas, any one or more of which may be particularly troublesome to you. It will also suggest which learning channel, the visual or the auditory, deserves special attention if you are to make maximum progress with a minimum of effort. Finally, it will suggest how much of a problem you have with proofreading.

So—go ahead with the test, checking your answers when you have finished.

SPELLING DIAGNOSTIC TEST

Each of the following sentences contains a potential spelling problem, including problems with hyphens and apostrophes. Spell each word in question in the space to the right of the sentence. Blank spaces call attention to trouble spots. Add any needed letter, letters, hyphens, or apostrophes to complete the spelling. With some, no letters or marks need be added to spell the word correctly. For example, confer___ence might be correctly spelled either by adding an *r* to make *conferrence* or by adding nothing to make *conference*. When you have three choices — *rain coat* / *rain-coat* / and *raincoat* — write the correct choice in the blank at the right.

Pay no attention to the numbers at the end of each line. They will be explained when you finish the test.

1. Try hop____g on the other foot. _____ (4)

2. He's our (quarter back / quarter-back / quarterback). _____ (12)

3. You can't fail — you're sure to suc_____. _____ (7)

1

4. Take your gr__vance to the boss. _____ (1)

5. I was still cons_____ after the accident. _____ (7)

6. They are writ__g a new set of rules. _____ (9)

7. What's that loud din__g noise I have been hearing? _____ (4)

8. Of the three cats, which is the livel__st? _____ (2)

9. The extra money benefit__ed them greatly. _____ (3)

10. Ther__s no reason to start the car. _____ (13)

11. Both attorn__s were in the office. _____ (11)

12. A baton twirler l__d the parade. _____ (14)

13. This room will a__commodate sixty students. _____ (10)

14. The teacher was hurr__ng upstairs. _____ (2)

15. Are you fr_____d or foe? _____ (1)

16. Is this a desir__able move to make? _____ (9)

17. I'm practic_____y certain to call tonight. _____ (8)

18. My son__-in-law__ car is parked at the far end of the driveway. _____ (13)

19. Follow the same proced_____ each time you place an order. _____ (6)

20. I'll take care of the matter personal_____y. _____ (8)

21. The plane is begin_____g to take off. _____ (3)

22. Great quantit_____s of supplies were missing. _____ (11)

23. The former idea is no better than the lat__er. _____ (4)

24. There goes my chemistry pro__fessor. _____ (10)

25. They have al__ready left for home. _____ (7)

26. I was plan_____g to visit my friend soon. _____ (4)

27. Put these papers into sep_____e folders. _____ (14)

28. I earned my livel_____hood by painting. _____ (2)

29. The loss of money was a dis__appointment. _____ (8)

30. The doctor will rel_____ve his pain. _____ (1)

2

31. The artist is an im__igrant from Italy. _____ (10)

32. Draw two paral__l lines on this page. _____ (14)

33. Get in front — you should pre_____ me in line. _____ (7)

34. I'm a for_____ner to this country. _____ (1)

35. The unexpected visit was quite a su__prise. _____ (5)

36. They spent a qu____t day in the country. _____ (1)

37. Let's make an (all out / all-out / allout) effort. _____ (12)

38. These FM radi_____s are less expensive. _____ (11)

39. The new ruling will a__fect only members. _____ (10)

40. First you're a freshman, then you're a soph_____re. _____ (5)

41. They left, but the_____ all coming back now. _____ (13)

42. There's Hill (High School / High-School / Highschool). _____ (12)

43. How many categor_____s are needed? _____ (11)

44. Am I bus_____r than you are? _____ (2)

45. In that morning class the at_____nce was poor. _____ (14)

46. I said I was definit____y interested. _____ (9)

47. After the seventh comes the _____th. _____ (1)

48. Telephone home to co_____roborate the facts. _____ (10)

49. Incident_____ly, I won't be able to go myself. _____ (8)

50. I acciden_____y lost my billfold. _____ (5)

51. Who_____ arriving on this flight? _____ (13)

52. I'm late. My watch keeps lo_____ time. _____ (9)

53. It's a (middle class / middle-class / middleclass) family. _____ (12)

54. I recently transfer____d into a new class. _____ (3)

55. The trapper was skin__g the bear. _____ (4)

56. Which car would you rec____mend
    buying? _____ (14)

57. A carpenter was plan____g the board to make
    it smooth. _____ (4)

58. She had an irresist__ble charm. _____ (6)

59. That point is i__relevant to the issue. _____ (10)

60. The princip__ reason is lack of time. _____ (7)

61. All six boy__ fathers came to help. _____ (13)

62. Did you rec__ve a letter from your friend? _____ (1)

63. It is a (two-lane / twolane / two lane) road. _____ (12)

64. This disclosure will embar____s the members
    of the organization. _____ (14)

65. My engineer is still handling plant
    mainten____nce. _____ (6)

66. That is a very a____propriate comment. _____ (10)

67. The prophet prophe____d this event. _____ (2)

68. It was a dis____ous train wreck. _____ (5)

69. I heard ech____ when I shouted. _____ (11)

70. The guests left the____ wraps in the hall
    closet. _____ (7)

71. This is an everyday occur____ence. _____ (3)

72. I looked at him cool__y, then turned away. _____ (8)

73. The ath____c director was in the gym. _____ (5)

74. I was sever__ly hurt in the crash. _____ (9)

75. This is a book about English gramm__. _____ (6)

76. Try stud__ng harder for the next exam. _____ (2)

77. Some schools tend to over-emphasize
    athleti____s. _____ (11)

78. Mark Twain's writings are very
    humor____ous. _____ (3)

79. My efforts were quite persist____nt. _____ (6)

80. It's a (light weight / light-weight /
    lightweight) cap. _____ (12)

4

81. My pal was in a sad state of drunken__ss. _____ (8)

82. If you____ tired, stay at home. _____ (13)

83. Dr. Smith is our most promin__nt authority. _____ (6)

84. The ruler tried to su____press the unwelcome
    news. _____ (10)

85. They were hop____g their friends would
    come. _____ (4)

86. The plane final__y arrived at the airport. _____ (8)

87. The appeal was an appar__nt failure. _____ (6)

88. Consult a good refer____ence work to find out. _____ (3)

89. Both sheriff__ were called to the scene. _____ (11)

90. How many pian__s did you sell today? _____ (11)

91. The dog led a miserable exist____ after that. _____ (6)

92. Slippery roads are a hin____ce when
    driving. _____ (5)

93. I ach____ved wide recognition as a speaker. _____ (1)

94. If you go to France, a passport is nec____sary. _____ (14)

95. The experiment was carefully control__d. _____ (3)

96. The key fit in the (key hole / key-hole /
    keyhole). _____ (12)

97. The dog lost it____ collar. _____ (13)

98. I noticed several mi____spelled words. _____ (8)

99. Now proc_____ with your report to the
    committee. _____ (7)

100. Come into the din____g room for lunch. _____ (4)

101. The exploring party was poorly equip____d. _____ (3)

102. Repeat it; rep____tion will produce
     results. _____ (14)

103. I must hurry or I will be late for my
     math____tics course. _____ (5)

104. The symphony ball was quite an oc_____sion. _____ (14)

105. The sun was shin_____g brightly. _____ (4)

106. I counted nin____y cars in the parking lot. _____ (9)

5

107. Who____ name did you call? _____ (7)

108. In the book, both her__s married heroines. _____ (11)

109. I'm carr____ng the tray to the table. _____ (2)

110. My prefer__ence is for classical piano music. _____ (3)

111. I have a new (rain coat / rain-coat / raincoat). _____ (12)

112. The smudge was hardly notic____able. _____ (9)

113. Did he lo____ his billfold in the struggle? _____ (7)

114. I worked in the chemical lab_____y. _____ (5)

115. It took a week____ time to finish the job. _____ (13)

116. This is for the conven____ce of our guests. _____ (1)

117. The preced____g reason seems clearer. _____ (9)

118. They had an arg____nt over the rules. _____ (9)

119. This is Charle__ new car. _____ (13)

120. Meet my new roo__mate. _____ (8)

121. Note the pron____tion of the word; then say it. _____ (7)

122. This requires special equip__ment. _____ (3)

123. Which actress portra____d the best part? _____ (2)

124. To get ahead, make yourself indispens__ble. _____ (6)

125. This is the bound__ry line for your lot. _____ (5)

126. I'm (college trained / college-trained / collegetrained). _____ (11)

127. Give us an exact d__scription of the fugitive. _____ (6)

128. I think it o__curred while you were away. _____ (10)

129. The child's lonel__ness was unbearable. _____ (2)

130. How many business____ went bankrupt? _____ (11)

131. The speaker used too many *and*____. _____ (13)

132. Insert the (mouth piece / mouth-piece / mouthpiece). _____ (12)

6

133. A large quan_____y of food was left over.   _____ (5)

134. Reading this in an hour takes real e__ficiency.   _____ (10)

135. I did the frog di__section in the lab.   _____ (8)

136. Did the applicant pos__s proper credentials?   _____ (14)

137. The child was bit__en on the ankle.   _____ (4)

138. We walked hurr__dly to the exit.   _____ (2)

139. Who is that I see com_____g down the street?   _____ (9)

140. You can hardly conc_____ve of its potential.   _____ (1)

KVCC Downtown Center
126 E. South Street
Kalamazoo, MI 49007

Now check your answers carefully, using the answer key on page 10. Circle the words you misspelled, including the number in parentheses that follows the spelling.

When you have checked all 140 items, tally your results using the appropriate boxes below. The boxes are numbered to correspond to the identifying numbers following each blank in the test. For each misspelling, note the identifying number after the blank and place a tally mark in the correspondingly numbered box, as in the sample.

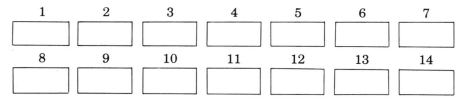

The box numbers correspond to the chapter numbers in this book. Thus, the sample indicates five errors of the kind covered in Chapter 12.

When you have completed your tally of errors, you can see your spelling problems at a glance. In the 140-item test, each of the 14 problem areas covered in the 14 chapters is represented by exactly 10 words. If you made five errors, for example, in any category, as in the sample box, you know you have missed exactly half of the test words for that particular problem.

Tally of Problem Areas

1	2	3	4	5	6	7

8	9	10	11	12	13	14

Look over your tally of problem areas. You can see — perhaps for the first time — the exact dimensions of your spelling problem. You now know what types of words are, for you, most troublesome to spell, which means you can concentrate your efforts so as to achieve best results.

But the diagnostic step you have just completed — important as it is — reveals only part of the picture. Sometimes you misspell words that you actually know how to spell. On a test of dictated words, one group of students scored 90 percent. When those same words appeared in a test such as you just took, the average remained fairly high: 80 percent. But — and here's the rub — when those same words appeared in a paragraph, the average dropped to about 60 percent. In short, if you learn how to spell a word but not how to proofread your spelling — or misspelling — your problem is still not solved. That's why you need to take the following additional diagnostic test — to check your proofreading accuracy.

PROOFREADING TEST

In the following passage underline all the spelling errors, including any involving a hyphen or apostrophe. Use the same care you would normally employ in correcting your own writing.

1   Actually, you have two mispelling problems: (1) spelling

2   words correctly as you write and (2) noticing incorrect

3   spellings as you proofread. Begining right now, start

4   studyng. Make a conscious effort to improve. Try

5   writting perfect papers. Faulty spelling is to much of

6   a handicap to be tolerated. It can be disasterous. Don't

7   let either you're eyes or ears decieve you. Check to see

8   which categorys in this text are most troublesome. Be

9   persistant. Be certian. Determine why you seem to have

10   trouble. Then proceed to take apropriate, well chosen

11   steps to remedy the situation. Here's hopping you make

12   excellent progress.

Check your answers with the key on page 11.

Answers to Diagnostic Test

1. hopping
2. quarterback
3. succeed
4. grievance
5. conscious
6. writing
7. dinning
8. liveliest
9. benefited
10. There's
11. attorneys
12. led
13. accommodate
14. hurrying
15. friend
16. desirable
17. practically
18. son-in-law's
19. procedure
20. personally
21. beginning
22. quantities
23. latter
24. professor
25. already
26. planning
27. separate
28. livelihood
29. disappointment
30. relieve
31. immigrant
32. parallel
33. precede
34. foreigner
35. surprise
36. quiet
37. all-out
38. radios
39. affect
40. sophomore
41. they're
42. High School
43. categories
44. busier
45. attendance
46. definitely
47. eighth
48. corroborate
49. Incidentally
50. accidentally
51. Who's
52. losing
53. middle-class
54. transferred
55. skinning
56. recommend
57. planing
58. irresistible
59. irrelevant
60. principal
61. boys'
62. receive
63. two-lane
64. embarrass
65. maintenance
66. appropriate
67. prophesied
68. disastrous
69. echoes
70. their
71. occurrence
72. coolly
73. athletic
74. severely
75. grammar
76. studying
77. athletics
78. humorous
79. persistent
80. lightweight
81. drunkenness
82. you're
83. prominent
84. suppress
85. hoping
86. finally
87. apparent
88. reference
89. sheriffs
90. pianos
91. existence
92. hindrance
93. achieved
94. necessary
95. controlled
96. keyhole
97. its
98. misspelled
99. proceed
100. dining
101. equipped
102. repetition
103. mathematics
104. occasion
105. shining
106. ninety
107. Whose
108. heroes
109. carrying
110. preference
111. raincoat
112. noticeable
113. lose
114. laboratory
115. week's
116. convenience
117. preceding
118. argument
119. Charles'
120. roommate
121. pronunciation
122. equipment
123. portrayed
124. indispensable
125. boundary
126. college trained
127. description
128. occurred
129. loneliness
130. businesses
131. *and's*
132. mouthpiece

133.	quantity	136.	possess	139.	coming
134.	efficiency	137.	bitten	140.	conceive
135.	dissection	138.	hurriedly		

Answers to Proofreading Test

You should have underlined the following 14 words and only those words. The correct form is provided in the second column. In this part of the test, one word from each of the 14 problem areas was introduced. Count as an error any misspelled word not underlined and any correctly spelled word underlined.

Spelling used	Correct spelling	Problem area	Percent missing word
mispelling (line 1)	misspelling	(8)	34%
begining (line 3)	beginning	(3)	29%
studyng (line 4)	studying	(2)	12%
writting (line 5)	writing	(9)	20%
to (line 5)	too	(7)	58%
disasterous (line 6)	disastrous	(5)	61%
you're (line 7)	your	(13)	27%
decieve (line 7)	deceive	(1)	31%
categorys (line 8)	categories	(11)	17%
persistant (line 9)	persistent	(6)	71%
certian (line 9)	certain	(14)	25%
apropriate (line 10)	appropriate	(10)	8%
well chosen (line 10)	well-chosen	(12)	90%
hopping (line 11)	hoping	(4)	39%

If you underlined words other than the 14 listed above, enter them in correctly spelled form on pages 132–133, with other personal spelling problems. Of those college students taking the proofreading test, 49 percent did not underline a single word that was correctly spelled. Thirty-eight percent underlined only one correctly spelled word, 8 percent underlined two, and 5 percent underlined three or four.

For you, just how much of a problem is proofreading? If you made four errors on the test, you have close to an average problem, and you are at the

56th percentile. Fewer than four errors and you are already well on the way to eliminating your proofreading problem. As many as 10 errors and you know you have a major problem. For you, this book should be indispensable. Use the following table to pinpoint the extent of your problem more exactly.

Number of errors	Percentile rank
0	100
1	97
2	89
3	75
4	56
5	40
6	29
7	23
8	12
9	6
10	3

As you can see, to spell well you must develop a kind of split personality — you the writer and you the proofreader. As you write, concentrate primarily on meaning, with spelling taking second place. After all, in that situation, meaning should come first, spelling second. But after you have finished writing, make a complete about-face and proofread what you've written. This time concentrate on spelling, with meaning taking second place. The more intently you focus on each role separately, the better you perform, both as writer and as proofreader.

The lower your proofreading percentile, the more important it is that you develop added proofreading skill. It pays off handsomely. Teachers, especially English teachers, have unusually well-developed proofreading skills, and misspelled words in a report or examination are apt to distract a teacher from the points you are trying to make. Gradually those misspellings build an image of you as either ignorant or careless — an unfortunate image for a student to have. On the other hand, a report or examination free or almost free of spelling errors is so unusual and so impressive that teachers may even over-rate your work. Skilled proofreading provides a real advantage and is a goal well worth striving for. Your task, then, is two-fold: (1) to learn how to spell, and (2) to learn how to proofread.

To help you develop this important skill, use the proofreading exercises at the end of each chapter. For example, if the tally shows that you have particular trouble with the *ei*/*ie* combinations, use the proofreading exercise at the end of Chapter 1 to full advantage. Work to develop a sharp visual image of the correct spelling. When writing, haven't you sometimes written several different spellings of a word to see which one looked right? If you rely on a visual image, it must be an accurate one. You must work to cultivate a clear, sharp image of the right spelling. Suppose you tend to misspell *receive* — you spell it *recieve,* with an *ie* instead of an *ei.* Look at the correct spelling. Shut your eyes and mentally go over each letter, especially the *cei* letters. Or say the rule to yourself "Write *i* before *e* except after *c.*" Note the *c* and fit your spelling to the rule to make the correction. Follow this procedure for a while and you'll soon find that you no longer need it. Your problem is solved. The right habits have been established.

To get a complete picture of yourself as a speller, use the profile sheets on pages 14 and 15. First, turn back to your tally of errors (p. 8). Since the test contained exactly 10 words in each category, subtract the number in each tally box from 10 to get the number of correct answers in each category. That's the number to enter on the profile sheets, in each of the numbered boxes at the top of the table. Also put a check in any box at the bottom for any words missed on the proofreading test, which contained one word from each category.

When you finish making these entries, you can make some helpful comparisons. Suppose you missed 3 of the 10 words in category 1. You enter a 7 — the number right — in the box under 1 on the profile sheet. Come down the column to the number 7 and underline it. Then look to the left to get your percentile rank: the 15th–18th percentile. This ranking means that for the category of *ie, ei* words, you have more than average difficulty, in comparison with a cross section of university students, and should take immediate steps to remedy it.

Compare your percentile on the Grand Total with your proofreading percentile (p. 12). Also compare your Auditory-Centered percentile with your Visual-Centered percentile. You'll then know yourself as a speller far better than most people, which means you can improve much more rapidly. After all, with that Profile Sheet before you, you know exactly what areas need emphasis.

To get your percentile rank, enter your scores in the appropriate boxes below. Then in each column, underline the number corresponding to the one in the box above. To get a spelling profile, connect the lines that you have made. For percentile ranks look along the line where the score is underlined to the column at the left of the page.

If your score in any of the columns is above the top dotted line, you're high in that area — among the top 25%. If any score is between the two dotted lines, you're average — among the middle 50%. If any score is below the bottom dotted line, you're low in that area — among the bottom 25%.

Part One   Auditory-Centered

(Enter numbers of words correctly spelled.)

%-ile	1	2	3	4	5	6	7	Total
95–99		10	10	10	10	10	10	62+
91–94	10					9	9	61
87–90								60
83–86				9				
79–82								59
75–78		9	9		9		8	58
71–74	9					8		57
67–70								56
63–66				8				55
59–62								
55–58		8						54
51–54					8		7	
47–50			8					53
43–46	8					7		52
39–42				7				51
35–38		7			7			50
31–34							6	
27–30								49
23–26		6	7			6		48
19–22				6	6			47
15–18	7						5	46
11–14		5			5	5		44–45
7–10	6		6	5				43
3–6	5	3–4	5	4	4	4		39–42
0–2	4	1–2	4	2–3	3	2–3		36–38

Proof-reading errors

Repeat the same procedure for the second part of the test, entering your scores below and connecting the underlined numbers to get your profile for this part of the test.

The grand total figure is, of course, the single best score for determining your overall spelling ability. Are you among the top 25%, the middle 50%, or the bottom 25%? No matter where you are, this text — rightly used — should bring immediate and welcome improvement.

Part Two   Visual-Centered

(Enter numbers of words correctly spelled.)

%-ile	8	9	10	11	12	13	14	Total	Grand Total
95–99	10	10		10	9–10	10	10	59+	119+
91–94	9		10	9	8			57–58	117–118
87–90						9			116
83–86		9					9	56	114–115
79–82						8		55	113
75–78	8				7			54	111–112
71–74			9	8				53	109–110
67–70							8	52	108
63–66								51	107
59–62		8				7		50	105–106
55–58					6				103–104
51–54	7						7	49	102
47–50								47–48	100–101
43–46			8	7				46	99
39–42									97–98
35–38		7			5	6		44–45	96
31–34							6	43	94–95
27–30	6								92–93
23–26					6			42	89–91
19–22		6	7		4	5		41	88
15–18							5	40	86–87
11–14	5	5						37–39	83–85
7–10			6	5	3	4		33–36	81–82
3–6	4	4	5	4		3	3–4	27–32	71–80
0–2	2–3	2–3	3–4	3	1–2	0–2	0–2	25–26	66–70

Proof-reading errors

Are you better at spelling or at proofreading? That's something worth knowing. To find out, get your Grand Total percentile rank from the Spelling Profile sheet. Then turn to page 12 and get your proofreading percentile rank. Compare the two and you'll know which needs most attention.

Then look at another aspect. Do you learn better by seeing or by hearing? Are you more eye-minded or ear-minded? The 14 problem areas are divided into auditory-centered and visual-centered categories to help answer these questions. The grouping was based largely on data from the *Brown-Carlsen Listening Comprehension Test*. Since spelling problems can be either auditory or visual, it should be particularly useful to know which category of problems you should emphasize. To find out, just compare your Total percentile for Part One with your Total percentile for Part Two.

For Part One, the best listeners made 24% *fewer* errors than the poorest listeners. For Part Two the best listeners made 32% *more* errors, suggesting a stronger visual element in test items for those seven categories. This is the first diagnostic test of spelling with attention sharply focused on the two channels — auditory and visual.

Actually, a problem well identified is a problem half solved. This means that when you've finished the diagnostic steps laid out in this section of the book, you will have taken the steps needed to obtain maximum results as you continue through the remainder of this text. Test results should also help you develop that spelling sixth sense — the when-to-reach-for-the-dictionary sense, so important both in proofreading and in regular spelling.

Each of the 14 problems isolated on the reading profile sheet is taken up in one of the chapters that follow, and the chapter numbers correspond to the numbers on the profile sheet.

PART ONE

Auditory-Centered Problems

1 Words with *ie, ei*

Do you wish to set your mind at ease about the correct spelling of over one thousand common words? Then memorize this bit of verse:

> Write **i** before **e**
> Except after **c**
> Or when sounded like **a**
> As in **neighbor** and **weigh**

Will this rule work for you all the time? Unfortunately not, but it will work for most of the words you are likely to have to spell on a day-to-day basis.

Let's examine the rule more closely, beginning with "**i** before **e** except after **c.**" This portion of the rule applies when the combination **ie** or **ei** is pronounced with a long **e**, the sound in **believe** or **field.** When the sound is a long **e**, you can, for the most part, spell the sound **ie**, except when it comes **immediately** after **c.** After **c,** reverse the combination to **ei.**

The instruction in this chapter, as in most of the chapters, is based upon programmed learning techniques. You are presented with a space into which you are to write an answer. The correct answer will usually appear to the left of the question. Learning occurs as you think about your answer and arrive at it unaided. You should refer to the answer given only as a means of checking your own reasoning processes. Don't short-circuit the system. Keep the answer column on the left covered with a piece of paper or cardboard until you have arrived at your own answer. Only in this way will you get the full benefit of programmed learning.

Try your hand with this list. If you miss one, go back and read the rule over again. Remember, cover the column on the left with a sheet of paper.

conceit   1. He was filled with conc____t.

conceive   2. How can you conc____ve of such an idea?

briefcase   3. She carried a br____fcase.

niece   4. His n___ce was an interesting woman.

chief   5. Did you play, "Doctor, lawyer, and Indian ch___f"?

receipt   6. Get a rec___pt for the money.

Now for the second half of the verse, "when sounded like an **a** as in **neighbor** and **weigh.**"

When the combination appears in words pronounced with the sound of **neighbor** or **weigh,** the correct spelling is **ei.** Try your hand at a few such words:

freight   1. The slow fr___ght came through town at

eight   ___ght o'clock.

reined   2. She r___ned in her horse.

vein   3. He hit a v___n of solid gold.

Now try a mixture that includes both the sounds of **piece** and **neighbor** and some **c** words like **conceit.**

ceiling   1. She painted the c___ling.

besieged   2. The movie star was bes___ged for autographs.

receive   3. It's better to give than to rec___ve.

chow mein   4. We had chow m___n for dinner.

sleigh   5. The sl___gh flew over the snow.

achieve   6. Work little, ach___ve little.

If you got all these words right, you are well on your way to spelling many tricky, common words correctly.

How about the exceptions to this rule? Well, to begin with, notice that the rule only applies when the **ie** or **ei** combination is a diphthong, that is, pronounced as one syllable as in **siege.** The rule does not apply when the combination spreads over two syllables as in **fiesta, science,** and **deity.** There is also a clue in the word **fiesta.** The rule does not always apply to words borrowed from foreign languages such as the French-derived **reveille.**

Other common words either not covered by the rule or exceptions to it are

ancient	Fahrenheit	leisure	sheik
caffeine	fiery	neither	sleight
codeine	financier	protein	stein
counterfeit	friend	seize	their
either	height	seizure	weird

Whenever you have trouble with an **ie** / **ei** word where the rule doesn't help, put it on your personal list of demons and memorize it. If your memory should fail you and a dictionary is not handy, remember this fact: two-thirds of all **ie** / **ei** words use **ie**. The odds are with you if you use **ie**.

(Circle all misspelled words in the passage below; then write the words correctly spelled into the numbered spaces provided. There may be more spaces provided than words misspelled. Finally, check your answers with the key that follows.)

In this brief exercise, try to percieve which words are

misspelled. I beleive a foreigner or alien would find that task

more difficult than your nieghbor. Such exercises are a cheif

way to develop added proofreading skill. Don't let word

appearances deceive you, and don't greive over mistakes.

Review this chapter if you achieve less than a perfect score.

Remember, exceptions to a rule are wierd.

1. _____ 2. _____ 3. _____

4. _____ 5. _____ 6. _____

7. _____ 8. _____ 9. _____

Key: 1. *perceive:* notice the *ei* which requires the *c* to follow **2.** *believe:* no *c* so you need the usual *ie* **3.** *neighbor:* notice the *a* sound which means *ei* also **4.** *chief:* the usual *ie,* the most common order **5.** *grieve* means *ei* also **6.** *weird:* one of those tricky exceptions (You might try a memory aid or *mnemonic* here, as explained in Chapters 6 and 14. A mnemonic for *weird,* for example, might be "Big Bird is weird.")

22

2 Final y

Why does **apology** become **apologies** but **attorney** become **attorneys**? Why does final **y** behave in different ways? For the answer, work through the following frames. (A helpful hint: in case you've forgotten, the alphabet is divided into vowels — *a, e, i, o, u,* sometimes *y* — and consonants — any letter not a vowel.)

1. The words **apology** and **attorney** both end in **y**, but in which word is the **y** preceded by a vowel?

attorney   In the word _____.

2. When an **s** is added to **attorney,** the combination is spelled **attorneys.** Similarly when an **s** is added to **alley,** you would expect the resulting

alleys   combination to be spelled how? _____

3. In the word **ally,** as in **apology,** the letter before the final **y** is a consonant. In this situation, to make a plural, think of the rhyme:

> With final **y**
> To gain success,
> Change **y** to **i**
> And add **es.**

Applying this rule, how would you spell the plural

allies   of **ally**? _____

4. When adding **-ed** to **ally,** follow the same procedure
allied   to get what spelling? _____

5. It is **allied** but **allying, rallied** but **rallying.** Of the two suffixes used in those words, which one
-ing   begins with an **i**? _____

6. Whenever a suffix beginning with an **i** is added to a word ending in **y**, keep the **y**, as in adding **-ing** to

steadying   **steady** to make the word _____.

7. The combination of **-er** and **steady** should,

steadier   however, be spelled how? _____

8. As a further aid, remember that in English words,
seldom   you (often/seldom) have two **i**'s right together.

9. Generally speaking, a consonant before the final **y** means changing the **y** to **i**, except with suffixes

i   beginning with what letter? _____

10. With suffixes beginning with any letter except **i**, either vowel or consonant, change **y** to what

i   letter? _____

11. Then there are a few long words where the **y** is even dropped. For example, this means that when you add **-ist** to **accompany,** you spell the resulting combination how?

accompanist   _____

12. For these long words, pronouncing them aloud — **accompanyist** vs. **accompanist** — should

y   remind you to drop the ____.

13. Pronounce **militaryism** and **militarism** and you

militarism   know that _____ is the correct spelling.

14. Now, how would you spell **vinegary + ish**?

vinegarish   _____

Think your way through the next 50 words, a sampling of those you can soon spell with real assurance. As usual, keep the answers covered until you're ready to check. If you misspell any word, make certain you know why — so it won't happen again.

trying	1. try + ing =	_____
murkiness	2. murky + ness =	_____
stayed	3. stay + ed =	_____
studying	4. study + ing =	_____
business	5. busy + ness =	_____
categorize	6. category + ize =	_____
loneliness	7. lonely + ness =	_____
varied	8. vary + ed =	_____
carrying	9. carry + ing =	_____
carrier	10. carry + er =	_____
ninetieth	11. ninety + eth =	_____
straying	12. stray + ing =	_____
merciful	13. mercy + ful =	_____
babying	14. baby + ing =	_____
application	15. apply + cation =	_____
funnier	16. funny + er =	_____
monkeyed	17. monkey + ed =	_____
allayed	18. allay + ed =	_____
holidaying	19. holiday + ing =	_____
beautiful	20. beauty + ful =	_____
weediness	21. weedy + ness =	_____
burial	22. bury + al =	_____
ceremonious	23. ceremony + ous =	_____

enjoying	24. enjoy + ing =	_____
fancied	25. fancy + ed =	_____
hungrier	26. hungry + er =	_____
jauntiest	27. jaunty + est =	_____
likeliest	28. likely + est =	_____
luxurious	29. luxury + ous =	_____
surveying	30. survey + ing =	_____
satisfied	31. satisfy + ed =	_____
storied	32. story + ed =	_____
theories	33. theory + es =	_____
tragedienne	34. tragedy + enne =	_____
tyrannical	35. tyranny + cal =	_____
keyed	36. key + ed =	_____
complying	37. comply + ing =	_____
follies	38. folly + es =	_____
employer	39. employ + er =	_____
angrily	40. angry + ly =	_____
luckily	41. lucky + ly =	_____
merriment	42. merry + ment =	_____
pitiful	43. pity + ful =	_____
studious	44. study + ous =	_____
marriage	45. marry + age =	_____
emptier	46. empty + er =	_____

prettiness   47. pretty + ness = _____

easily   48. easy + ly = _____

dignifying   49. dignify + ing = _____

busily   50. busy + ly = _____

(Circle all misspelled words in the passage below; then write the words, correctly spelled, in the numbered spaces provided. There may be more spaces provided than words misspelled. Finally, check your answers with the key that follows.)

Tip: First look for all words ending in **y** before the suffix is added. Then check each word by rule to see if it is spelled correctly.

Try employing this exercise to check your mastery of the chap-

ter on the final *y*. Keep studiing busily until you're satisfied

with the results. Concentrate on those word categories causing

most trouble. With practice, spelling should come more easyly,

with the likelyhood of errors greatly reduced. Turn theorys to

practical application. And don't be too hurryed as you work

along. Identifyng misspellings is trickier than trying to spell

the same words from dictation. Remember, laziness gets you

nowhere!

1. _____   2. _____   3. _____

4. _____   5. _____   6. _____

7. _____   8. _____   9. _____

Key: 1. *studying*: seldom two *i*'s together 2. *easily*: *y* is preceded by a consonant 3. *likelihood*: *y* is preceded by a consonant 4. *theories*: change *y* to *i* and add *es* 5. *hurried*: *y* is preceded by a consonant 6. *identifying*: to avoid two *i*'s together

3 The Final Consonant Rule

Why double the **r** in **referred** but not in **reference**?
Here's a rule to answer that question — perhaps the most useful spelling
rule of all. With it, you can spell, not 300, but 3,000 fairly common words.
That's right! Master one rule — spell 3,000 words. Furthermore, you can use
it with a minimum of worry for it has so few exceptions.

Now for the rule:

Words (1) *ending in a single final consonant,* (2) *preceded by a single
vowel,* **double the final consonant** when (3) *a suffix beginning with a
vowel is added* and when (4) *the last syllable is accented.*

To be sure, that's a bit complicated. But you can make it easier by
remembering this sentence: A fourfold check saves a pain in the neck. And
here's that check:

(1) Is there a *single final consonant?*
(2) Is there a *single preceding vowel?*
(3) Does the suffix to be added *begin with a vowel?*
(4) Is the *last syllable accented?*

When the word checks out completely, **double the final consonant.**

Again, use the programmed approach to speed your progress. Keep those
answers in the left-hand margin covered until you've filled in the blanks.
Then check by uncovering them. If you miss one, rethink it. You want
complete mastery of this indispensable rule.

begin

1. Of the words **begin, end,** and **race,** which one ends in

   a single final consonant? _____

sin

2. Of the words **rein, seen,** and **sin,** which has a single
   vowel before the single final consonant?

   _____

3. Of the words **begin, listen,** and **enter,** which is accented on the last syllable? _____

beGIN

4. Of the suffixes **-ness, -ly,** and **-ing,** which begins with a vowel? _____

-ing

5. Since **beGIN** (a) ends in a single final consonant, (b) is preceded by a single vowel, and (c) is accented on the last syllable, when you add the suffix **-ing,** which begins with a vowel, you should spell the resulting combination _____.

beginning

6. Try that fourfold check to see how to spell the combination **enter + -ing.**

   (a) Does **enter** end in a single final consonant? _____

(a) yes

   (b) Is the consonant **r** preceded by a single vowel? _____

(b) yes

(c) no
   (c) Is the last syllable accented? _____

(d) yes
   (d) Is **-ing** a suffix beginning with a vowel? _____

   Only if you answered "yes" to all four questions do you double the final consonant. Now spell

entering
   enter + -ing = _____.

7. When you add **-ed** to **occur,** you should spell the

occurred
   resulting combination _____.
   (If you missed this, run through the fourfold check to see why).

8. In words containing a **qu** letter combination, such as **quip, quit,** and **quiz,** the **qu** has the sound of **kw.** The word **quiz,** for example, sounds as if it were

k**w**iz
   spelled k___iz.

9. In the word **quiz,** since the **qu** has the sound of **kw,** you have a single vowel, so you apply the rule when

quizzed
   you add **-ed** to **quiz** to make _____.

10. Now how would you spell **quit + -ing?** Give it the

30

usual fourfold check. Remember **qu** is pronounced

quitting

kw. _____

11. How would you spell the combination **quiet + -er?**

quieter

_____

suffix (only **-est**
begins with
a vowel)

12. What explains the difference in spelling between
fattest and **fatness?** (a) accent, (b) suffix, or

(c) final consonant? _____

13. What explains the difference in spelling between
planning and **planking?** (a) accent, (b) suffix, (c)
vowel, or (d) final consonant?

final
consonant

_____

14. What explains the difference in spelling between
meeting and **betting?** (a) accent, (b) suffix, (c)
vowel, or (d) final consonant?

vowel

_____

15. What explains the difference in spelling between **referred** and **reference?** (a) accent, (b) suffix, (c)
vowel, or (d) final consonant?

accent
(re**FERR**ed vs.
REFerence)

_____

16. Spell the combination **humor + -ous.**

humorous

_____

(Note the accented syllable.)

17. How do you spell **depend + -ent?**

dependent

_____

controlled

18. Spell **control + -ed.** _____

occurrence

19. Spell **occur + -ence.** _____

20. Now for important exceptions. Since **TRANSfer** is
preferably accented on the first syllable, when you
add **-ed** or **-ing,** you should, by rule, spell the
resulting combination by (1) doubling or (2) not

not doubling

doubling the final consonant?_____

21. But this is a major exception. Use a memory aid. With **TRANSfer,** mentally **transFER** the accent to the other syllable and then apply the rule. The correct spelling of **transfer + -ed** is

transferred

_____.

22. The other important exceptions are **excellent** and **excellence.** Again, use a mnemonic. When you excel, you "go beyond" the usual. That means in

beyond

spelling those words, you should "go _____" the usual single **l** when you add **-ent** or **-ence.**

23. In summary, the most important exceptions to the final consonant rule are the words

transferred,
transferring,
excellent, and
excellence

_____, _____,

_____, and

_____.

Now extend your application of this rule by working through the next 40 words, a small sampling of the thousands of words you can soon spell easily and accurately. Again, keep the correct spelling to the left covered until you're ready to check — a fourfold check.

With this rule a common problem is knowing which syllable is accented. Here's a helpful suggestion. Try overemphasizing each syllable. For example, say **COMmit,** with a really strong accent on **COM.** Then try it the other way — **comMIT.** Which sounds more natural? **COMmit** sounds strange. **ComMIT** sounds better. So — the accent belongs on the last syllable.

committee

1. commit + ee = _____

controlled

2. control + ed = _____

compelling

3. compel + ing = _____

occurrence

4. occur + ence = _____

benefited

5. benefit + ed = _____

thinner

6. thin + er = _____

forgotten

7. forgot + en = _____

goddess	8. god + ess =	_____
marvelous	9. marvel + ous =	_____
regretful	10. regret + ful =	_____
propellant	11. propel + ant =	_____
hopping	12. hop + ing =	_____
conference	13. confer + ence =	_____
rebellion	14. rebel + ion =	_____
spinner	15. spin + er =	_____
submitting	16. submit + ing =	_____
fogged	17. fog + ed =	_____
exceeded	18. exceed + ed =	_____
outmanned	19. outman + ed =	_____
pocketed	20. pocket + ed =	_____
commitment	21. commit + ment =	_____
beginner	22. begin + er =	_____
referral	23. refer + al =	_____
travelogue	24. travel + ogue =	_____
preference	25. prefer + ence =	_____
interested	26. interest + ed =	_____
equipped	27. equip + ed =	_____
transmitting	28. transmit + ing =	_____
winning	29. win + ing =	_____
transferred	30. transfer + ed =	_____
different	31. differ + ent =	_____

KVCC KALAMAZOO VALLEY COMMUNITY COLLEGE LIBRARY

planned	32. plan + ed =	_____
gagged	33. gag + ed =	_____
repellent	34. repel + ent =	_____
baggage	35. bag + age =	_____
ripping	36. rip + ing =	_____
reaped	37. reap + ed =	_____
robbed	38. rob + ed =	_____
lemonade	39. lemon + ade =	_____
excellent	40. excel + ent =	_____

PROOFREADING EXERCISE

(Circle all misspelled words in the passage below; then write the words, correctly spelled, in the numbered spaces provided. There may be more spaces provided than words misspelled. Finally, check your answer with the key that follows.)

Begining here, circle each misspelled occurrence. To be

benefitted as you should, work clear through this carefully

planned and controled exercise. Be consistent in applying the

rule. Otherwise you won't be properly equiped for proofreading

excelence.

1. _____ 2. _____ 3. _____

4. _____ 5. _____ 6. _____

Key: 1. beginning 2. benefited 3. controlled 4. equipped 5. excellence

4 **Vowel Length**

It's just a short step from the final consonant rule to another principle, useful in dealing with words ending in silent **e.** For example, you already know how to pronounce **pet** and **Pete, pin** and **pine.** The silent **e** changes the preceding vowel from short to long. How do you put that knowledge to use in spelling another sizable group of words?

Can you discover for yourself the principle that applies? Again, use a programmed approach. Cover the answers on the left and start right in.

1. When you add a silent **e** to **rat,** to make **rate,** you change the pronunciation of **a** from short to

long   _____ .

2. And when you add a silent **e** to **red** to make that strange word **rede,** would you expect **rede** to

seed   rhyme with **led** or **seed?** _____

3. A silent **e** after **fin** would change the short **i** to a

long   _____ **i.**

4. How would you lengthen the vowel in the word **hop** to make a word rhyming with soap? Add a silent

e   _____ .

5. How would you shorten the vowel in **cute?** By removing the _____ .
silent *e*

6. As you can see, noting the relationship between a
vowel   terminal silent **e** and _____ length should improve your spelling.

7. If you **dine** and **wine** someone, how would you spell

those same words with an **-ing** added, as in

dining; wining

d____ing and w____ing someone?

8. If there is a **din** when you **win** a special award, how would you spell those same words with an **-ing**

dinning; winning

added? d____ing and w____ing

9. Think of vowel length and the silent **e** as you add **-ing**

canning

to the following words: One was can ____ peas while

caning

the other was can____ a chair seat.

10. Add **-ed** to **tap** and **tape** in the following context: She

tapped (tap + -ed)

_____ the pipe that was heavily

taped (tape + -ed)

_____.

11. Add **-ing** to **grip** and **gripe** in the following context:

gripping

One was _____ the rope while the other was

griping

_____ about the heat.

staring
(stare + -ing)
starring
(star + -ing)

12. Add **-ing** to **stare** and **star** in the following context: The child was _____ at the picture of the _____ actress.

mopping
(mop + -ing)
moping
(mope + -ing)

13. Fit the needed words into this context: A worker got the **mop** and was _____ the floor while a dejected friend was _____ about the pay.

scared
(scare + -ed)
scarred
(scar + -ed)

14. Fit **scar** and **scare** into this context: They were _____ to death by the ghost with the badly _____ hand.

keep

15. Now you know why there is a final consonant rule. That doubling of the final consonant is a necessary move to (change / keep) the vowel length the same, as in **bar** and **barring**.

Now to make sure that you have learned when to double the final consonant, here are some more examples. Your answer will be determined by the vowel length. Some of the words will require no additional letter.

filed; filled

1. As they fil____ed the cards, they fil____ed the entire drawer.

dinning; dining

2. He heard the din____ing noise in the din____ing room.

spitting; spiting

3. You're spit____ing just to be spit____ing me.

pining; pinning

4. The officer was pin____ing to be pin____ing the speaker down to the facts.

griped; gripped

5. One grip____ed while the other grip____ed the handle.

gaping; gapping

6. She was gap____ing through the gap____ing hole.

sparing

sparring

7. In the ring, the boxer was not spar____ing his spar____ing partner.

tapping

taping

8. The runner heard the tap__ing sound while tap__ing a sore ankle.

lamed; lammed

9. The player lam____ed himself when he lam____ed the baseball over the fence and tripped.

slopping

sloping

10. The water which was slop____ing out of the can was running down the slop____ing terrace.

cutter; cuter

11. The girl who was the meat cut____er was cut____er than anyone else.

latter

later

12. Of the two, Sue and Carol, the lat____er was the lat____er in arriving.

13. When the dynamite arrived, the miner began

fussing; fusing

fus____ing over the fus____ing.

riding

ridding

14. The cowboy was rid__ing away in hopes of rid____ing himself of added responsibility.

shining; shinning 15. The sun was shin____ing as he was shin____ing up the pole.

planning; planing 16. The owner was plan____ing on plan____ing the board in the new workshop.

hopping

hoping

17. As she was hop____ing down the hill, she was hop____ing not to sprain her ankle.

bite; bit 18. With each bit____ the dog ate only a little bit____ of meat.

wager; wagger 19. I wag____er that dog is the best tail wag____er there is.

dinner; diner 20. On the train she had din____er in the din____er.

PROOFREADING EXERCISE

(Circle all misspelled words in the following passage; then write the words, correctly spelled, in the numbered spaces provided. There may be more spaces provided than words misspelled. Finally, check your answers with the key that follows.)

We're hopping that you're winning your battle against poor

spelling. Every chapter should help in ridding yourself of

another problem. Sooner or latter you won't need to be mopping

around the house, gripping, fussing and fuming about your

spelling. We wager that even now your writen work is

beginning to be a bright and shining example of excellence,

thanks to your careful planning and study.

1. _____   2. _____   3. _____

4. _____   5. _____   6. _____

Key: 1. hoping 2. later 3. mopping 4. gripping 5. written

38

5 Pronunciation Difficulties

Speakers of English, both in Great Britain and in America, are notoriously lazy about the pronunciation of their language. They are seldom reluctant to drop out vowels, consonants, indeed, whole syllables, when such dropping eases the pronunciation of a word. Through such practices, **Gloucester** is pronounced **Gloster, forecastle** is pronounced **fo'c's'le, Worcestershire** becomes **woostershir, forehead** becomes **forrid,** and so forth. Also common in English is the practice of representing the same sound by different combinations of letters. **Pane** rhymes with **vein** and **write** with **right** despite the spelling differences. And we do the reverse. The same letter combinations can represent different sounds. **Tough** does not rhyme with **cough,** and neither rhymes with **although,** in spite of their all containing the **ough** spelling. The playwright George Bernard Shaw, a great advocate of spelling reform, pointed out these inconsistencies by spelling fish **ghoti.** He used the **gh** from **tough,** the **o** from **women,** and the **ti** from **addition.**

Such confusing uses of the various letter combinations in English lead some people to throw up their hands in despair and to decide that pronunciation can never be a key to spelling in English. In part, such people are right. Nevertheless, a good many people misspell a great many words simply because they are sloppy with their pronunciation. They misspell **incidentALLY,** for example, because they mispronounce it as **incidentLY,** or misspell **govERNment** because they mispronounce it as **govERment.**

This chapter will deal with a number of common words that are often mispronounced and therefore misspelled.

Exercise

Following each word write the correct pronunciation as recorded in your desk or college dictionary. Then, while saying the word aloud, spell it correctly in the two blanks. Learn to associate sound with spelling in this group of words. In the first column we have placed the correct pronunciation for each word as recorded in our dictionary. (For your convenience an abbreviated pronunciation key is placed at the bottom of page 41.)

You could work this exercise using our pronunciations and our pronunciation key, but we advise you to use your own dictionary. By doing so, you will not only learn the correct pronunciation, but will learn as well how to check the pronunciation of any word in your dictionary. Possibly, the pronunciation we give you may be slightly different from the pronunciation you find in your dictionary. If you are working with a good dictionary, don't let this slight difference trouble you.

Sample

feb′ roo-er-i   February   *feb′roo-er-i   February*
                                                   February

Notice the boldface **r** in our spelling of **February.** The **r** is the trouble spot in **February** because so many people mispronounce it as **feb oo-er-i.** The trouble spots in all the words in this exercise will appear in boldface. We will also occasionally provide notes that further clarify the spelling of a word.

ak-sə-den′ t′l-i   1. accidentally   _____   _____
                                                                      _____

ak′yoo-rə-si   2. accuracy   _____   _____
                                                                      _____

ə-kwīr′   3. acquire   _____   _____
                                                                      _____

ärk′ tik   4. arctic   _____   _____
                                                                      _____

as′ pēr-in   5. aspirin   _____   _____
                                                                      _____

ath-let′iks   6. athletics   _____   _____
                                                                      _____

ô-then′tik   7. authentic   _____   _____
                                                                      _____

40

bās′i-k′l-i   8. basically   _____ _____

_____

Most adjectives ending in **ic** form the adverb by adding **ally**. **Publicly** is one of the few exceptions.

boun′də-ri   9. bound**ary**   _____ _____

dif′ ēr-ənt   10. diff**erent**   _____

di-zas′trəs   11. disast**rous**   _____

_____

Disastrous is commonly misspelled because the writer takes the noun **disaster** and adds an **ous** to it, ending up with **disasterous.** Four other words are commonly misspelled for similar reasons: **entrance (enter), hindrance (hinder), monstrous (monster),** and **remembrance (remember).**

en′trəns   12. ent**rance**   _____ _____

_____

in-vī′rən-mənt   13. enviro**nm**ent   _____ _____

_____

guv′ērn-mənt   14. gover**nm**ent   _____ _____

_____

grēv′əs   15. grie**vous**   _____ _____

_____

Abbreviated Pronunciation Key

hat, tāpe, bâre, cär; end, ēvening, hêre, ovēr; his, whīte; got, gō, hôrn, fool, cook, soil, out; up, ūse, fūr; get; joy; yet; child; show; thin; zh, leisure; ng, sing; 'as in table (ta b'l); ə known as the schwa, used for the weakened uh sound found in such words as about, regent, locus. (This sound can be represented by any vowel and therefore is very troublesome in spelling. See Chapter 6).

hīt   16. height   _____ _____
                                                        _____

hin'drəns   17. hindrance   _____ _____
                                                        _____

in-si-den't'l-i   18. incidentally   _____ _____
                                                        _____

lab'ēr-ə-tō-ri   19. laboratory   _____ _____
                                                        _____

Remember that scientists **labor** in their **laboratory**.

lī'brer-i   20. library   _____ _____
                                                        _____

luk'shə-ri   21. luxury   _____ _____
                                                        _____

math-ə-mat'iks   22. mathematics   _____ _____
                                                        _____

min'i-ə-chər   23. miniature   _____ _____
                                                        _____

mon'strəs   24. monstrous   _____ _____
                                                        _____

pärt'nēr   25. partner   _____ _____
                                                        _____

kwän'tə-ti   26. quantity   _____ _____
                                                        _____

ri-mem'brəns   27. remembrance   _____ _____
                                                        _____

sēn′ēr-i   28. scenery _____ _____

                _____

sof′ə-môr   29. sophomore _____ _____

                _____

sēr-prīz′   30. surprise _____ _____

                _____

tem′pēr-ə-mənt 31. temperament _____ _____

                _____

tem′pēr-ə-chēr 32. temperature _____ _____

                _____

um-brel′ə   33. umbrella _____ _____

                _____

Many other words besides the 33 words you have just worked through are troublesome because of sloppy pronunciation. Some examples follow, with the letter often omitted printed as a capital: **attempT, canDidate, chocOlate, considErable, hanDsome, idenTical, literAture, prompTly,** and **recoGnize.**

When you add a word to your own list of demons, determine if you have trouble with it because of pronunciation. If you do, look up its pronunciation in a good desk dictionary and write it several times as you pronounce it aloud.

Now check yourself on the words you have just worked through. Have somebody whose pronunciation is reliable read you the words on the list as you spell them. If you have access to a tape recorder, you can record your own list and play it back for yourself. If you miss any, go back to them and be sure you are pronouncing them correctly. Write and say aloud each word you missed at least ten times.

(Circle all misspelled words in the passage below; then write the words correctly spelled into the numbered spaces provided. There may be more spaces provided than words misspelled. Finally, check your answers with the key that follows.)

Absorbed in his enterance, the performer playing Hamlet stumbled while ascending the stairs to Gertrude's room. He dropped the sword he was carrying, and it made a continous clanging as it rolled down the stairs. Prespiration rolled down the actor's face as he picked himself up from the floor.

"At your convenence," shouted the director, "can we go back to playing this as a tragedy?"

1. _____ 2. _____ 3. _____

4. _____ 5. _____ 6. _____

7. _____ 8. _____ 9. _____

In this exercise, if you miss some of the misspelled words or mark as incorrect words that are correctly spelled, you may not be pronouncing them accurately. Check the pronunciations in a reliable dictionary and relate them to the correct spelling of the words.

Key: 1. entrance 2. continuous 3. perspiration 4. convenience

44

6 Unstressed Vowels

When we come to the problem of unstressed vowels in English, we come to a real stumbling block. In the last chapter we told you how speakers of English were notoriously lazy in their pronunciation of the language. We brought up the subject at that time to warn you against mispronunciations that could lead you to misspellings. But, if enough people are lazy enough about the pronunciation of a word for a long enough time, the lazy pronunciation becomes the accepted one. The habit of not giving vowels their full value while pronouncing them — a habit that results in unstressed vowels — has gone on in English for centuries. As a result, English has thousands of words in which proper pronunciation is an incomplete guide to spelling.

For example, the **able** in **desirable** is pronounced the same as the **ible** in **incredible.** The **ant** in **relevant** is pronounced like the **ent** in **prevalent.** Unstressed vowels are found everywhere in our words: in prefixes such as **de-(develop), di-(dilute),** and **dis-(discipline).** In suffixes such as **-ant (tolerant), -ent (accident), -able (acceptable), -ible (flexible), -ar (dollar), -er (hunger), -ir (elixir), -or (terror),** and **-ur (murmur).** And in the middle of words, as in **cemEtery** and **sepArate.**

In dictionary pronunciation keys, the unstressed vowels are most generally represented by the **schwa** (ə), an upside-down **e.** The *schwa* is given a soft *uh* sound like the final sound in **sofa.** Unfortunately, in spelling, the sound can be represented by any of the vowels (**a, e, i, o, u**), even **y,** as in **synonYmous.** The other most common unstressed sound is the **i** sound found in such words as **solId, privAte, knowlEdge,** and **benefIt.**

What are you, the put-upon speller, to do about this stickler of a problem? Well, to begin with, being aware of the problem is perhaps the most important thing for you. Develop a healthy sense of doubt whenever you spell words that contain unstressed vowels. When you wish to express the state of existing, look it up in the dictionary to be sure it is, indeed, **existence** and not **existance.**

Another aid to use is the *mnemonic.* A mnemonic (pronounced ni-mon'ik) is a device used to jog your memory, usually an association trick of some sort. Many words with unstressed vowels can be spelled correctly by associating them with words with the same root where the troublesome vowel is given its full value. For example, the **o** in **authOr** is unstressed, but in **authOrity** it is clearly an **o.** Similar associations can be had with **defInite** and **defIne, grammAr** and **grammAtical, oppOsite** and **oppOse,** and **tolerAnt** and **tolerAte.** This particular mnemonic will work for hundreds of words. Remember, too, that there are families of words in which all forms have unstressed vowels, but where if you can spell one word in the family, you have the spelling of a variant form. If you can spell **evidEnt** correctly with an **e,** you can also fearlessly spell **evidEnce** with an **e.** Likewise with **intelligEnt** and **intelligEnce, IndependEnt** and **independEnce, dEscribe** and **dEscription,** and so forth.

When no family associations exist to help you spell a word, you can make up mnemonics of your own. Can you never remember that the second vowel sound in **sepArate** is an **a?** Then perhaps a sentence like, "Agatha is **sepArated** from John" may stick in your head. "To **profess or** not to profess, that is the question" may help you to remember the correct spelling of **professor.** Remembering that "the **villain** is **in** his **villa**" may keep you from misspelling the word as **villian.**

For many such words you may simply have to resort to memorization. Write the troublesome word about 10 times, capitalizing the unstressed letter or letters. It may help if you say the word aloud at the same time giving the unstressed vowel its full value (even though you know it's not pronounced that way). After you have memorized the word, try for a few weeks to work it into your writing as often as you can, until you can spell it with confidence.

Following is a list of common words containing unstressed vowels that tests indicate people frequently misspell. The list is broken down into family groups, depending upon whether the principal unstressed vowel is an **a, e, i, o, u,** or **y.** When mnemonic words are available, they are included. You may wish to make up some mnemonics of your own. Learn all the words on the list through the use of mnemonics or memorization. When you are confident that you know all the words, have someone read you the test list that follows the learning list. Return to the learning list as many times as necessary until you have mastered all the words on it.

But do remember that these words constitute a very partial listing of the thousands of words that contain unstressed vowels. Be aware of the problem and keep that dictionary handy.

LEARNING LIST

A

acceptAble
amAteur
appearAnce
calEndAr
desirAble
embarrAss
explAnation
grammAr (grammAtical)
guidAnce
hangAr
indispensAble
librAry (librArian)
magAzine
maintEnAnce
marriAge
peaceAble
prevAlEnt
relEvAnt
respectAble
sepArate
tolErAnt (tolerAte)
vulgAr (vulgArian)

I

defInite (defIne)
dIscipline
dIsease
dIvide
dIvine
elIgIble
incredIble
irresistIble
medIcine
orIgInal
rIdiculous

U

murmUr
procedUre
pUrsue

E

absEnce
accidEnt
apparEnt
arithmEtic (arithmEtical)
benEfit
catEgory
cemEtEry
consistEnt
dEscription
differEnce
efficIEnt
exaggErate
excellEnt
existEnce
experiEnce
experimEnt
independEnce
intelligEnce
licEnse
occurrEnce
persistEnt
privilEge
promillEnt

O

actOr
memOry (memOrial)
neighbOr
professOr

Y

martYr

absence
acceptable
accident
actor
amateur
apparent
appearance
arithmetic
benefit
calendar
category
cemetery
consistent
definite
description
desirable
difference
discipline
disease
divide
divine
efficient

eligible
embarrass
exaggerate
excellent
existence
experience
experiment
explanation
grammar
guidance
hangar
incredible
independence
indispensable
intelligence
irresistible
library
license
magazine
martyr
maintenance
marriage

medicine
memory
murmur
neighbor
occurrence
peaceable
original
persistent
prevalent
privilege
procedure
professor
prominent
pursue
relevant
respectable
ridiculous
separate
tolerant
vulgar

NAME _____ DATE _____

(Circle all misspelled words in the passage below; then write the words correctly spelled into the numbered spaces provided. There may be more spaces provided than words misspelled. Finally, check your answers with the key that follows.)

"To hopefully live," began the student in a murmering voice.

"Stop," roared the professor. "I do not exaggarate when I say

your grammer is ridiculous." With that, the professor whipped

out a cutlass and sliced the student in two.

"There," the professor said, "is a marter to the split infinitive."

The other students were greatly embarrassed by the professor's

behavior. They did not object to his sword play, but they

thought his word play defied discription.

1. _____   2. _____   3. _____

4. _____   5. _____   6. _____

7. _____   8. _____   9. _____

When you miss words in this group, remember to keep that healthy sense of doubt about words that have unstressed vowels in them. You'll have to check them out in the dictionary. For some, you can make up mnemonics, such as "I'll murmur U if you'll murmur me."

Key: 1. murmuring 2. exaggerate 3. grammar 4. martyr 5. description

7 Sound-Alikes

Many words in English are pronounced identically, or nearly so, to other words with different spellings and different meanings — words such as **weather** and **whether,** for example. To say the least, this likeness creates a problem for the conscientious speller. Since there is often no clue to the correct spelling in the pronunciation of the word, the speller must key in on meaning. In the examples that follow we will deal with the most common of these troublesome words (there are many others). We will present the word and its meaning and use it in a sentence for you. Then we will give you an opportunity to use it correctly. Only by firmly connecting the meaning of the word with the correct spelling can you hope to do well with this group of words.

Remember to keep the left column covered as you work your way through the examples.

1. **accept** — to take what is offered. She **accepted** the $500 scholarship.

   except — excluding or leaving out (*usually a preposition, but is also a verb*).
   Everyone, **except** me, went to the play.

accept

except

   Do you _____ candy from strangers?

   We had a good time, _____ for the weather.

2. **advice** — an opinion or counsel (*a noun*). She gave her son good **advice.**

   advise — to give advice (*a verb*). He **advised** the general to surrender.

advised

advice

   My father _____ me never to lend money to men in striped suits.

   I took my father's _____ and saved a lot of money.

3. **affect** — to influence, to produce a change or an effect. My father's advice **affected** my whole life.

effect — something brought about, a result (*noun*). Susan's smile had an amazing **effect** on Jim. The word may also be *a verb* meaning "to bring about." Having a child **effected** a big change in Jim.

Did winning all that money have any

effect

_____ on her personality?

affect

No, winning the money did not _____ her personality a bit.

effect

However, winning the money did _____ a change in her shopping habits.

4. **already** — by or before some given or implied time. He was **already** in his seat by the time the curtain went up.

all ready — completely prepared. He was **all ready** to go after he found his theater tickets.

already

Mary was _____ a fine athlete by the age of twelve.

Except for a missing sleeping bag, she was

all ready

_____ to go on her camping trip.

all right — **all right,** meaning satisfactory or adequate, really doesn't sound like **all ready,** but we thought we would mention it here. By analogy with **already,** some people spell **all right** as **alright.** Don't! **Alright** is still considered a substandard spelling by most people.

5. **all together** — in a group. The boys stood **all together** in the corner.

altogether — wholly, completely. The President was not **altogether** pleased with the election results.

all together

The family was _____ every Christmas.

altogether

The coach was not _____ happy with her team's loss.

6. **an** — along with **a** the indefinite article. **An** apple a day keeps the doctor away.

and — the conjunction. My wife **and** I lived all alone.

and

an

Charlie _____ I went to school together.

We had only ____ hour to get ready.

7. **capital** — chief, important (*adjective*); wealth, money (*noun*); actually, any use of the word except for the very restricted use that refers to the building where a legislature meets. The inventor lacked the **capital** needed to finance his invention.

Capitol — the building where the United States Congress meets or (usually with a small **c**) the building where a state legislature meets. There is a small subway that connects the **Capitol** with an office building. (But note well that the **Capitol** is located in the **capital,** which is Washington, D.C.)

The state legislature has its offices and meeting

capitol

rooms in the _____.

capital

He thought the idea to paint the **Capitol** red, white, and blue was a _____ notion.

Notice that the **Capitol** in Washington is spelled

capital

with a _____ **C.**

8. **choose** — to pick or to select. Did Dave **choose** the brown suit or the blue?

chose — past tense of **choose.** He **chose** the blue suit.

choose

I do not _____ to run for reelection.

chose

All too often in the past people _____ convenience over environmental safety.

9. **clothes** — wearing apparel, garments. The **clothes** that people wear reflect their personalities.

cloths — two or more pieces of cloth. The white **cloths** used as flags of truce fluttered everywhere in the captured city.

People in business have to choose their

clothes

_____ carefully.

dishcloths

Have dish _____ been completely replaced by dishwashers?

53

10. **complement** — something that completes (*noun*) or to make complete (*verb*). His dirty white sneakers **complemented** his faded blue jeans.

    compliment — praise (*noun*) or to give praise (*verb*).

    He **complimented** the cook for his marvelous food.

    By filling in needed detail, the second book

complemented   _____ the first.

compliment   Everyone appreciates a sincere

     _____.

11. **council** — a group of advisers, a governing body. The mayor and her **council** meet every Tuesday.

    counsel — advice, also a lawyer (*noun*), to give advice (*verb*). Mother's **counsel** to my sister was to go to college.

council   The Congress is a governing _____.

counseled   My lawyer _____ me to remain quiet in court.

counsel   I took his _____ and stayed out of jail.

12. **foreword** — a preface to a piece of writing. His old professor wrote the **foreword** to his book.

    forward — ahead or in front. Please move **forward** in the bus.

forward   "_____," the general urged his troops.

foreword   The Secretary of the Interior wrote the _____ to the book on conservation.

13. **hear** — to take in sound through the ear. From the back of the theater he could not **hear** the actors.

    here — present at this place. Nick was **here** all morning.

here   She was _____, there, and everywhere.

hear   Can you _____ me back there?

14. **its** — possessive form of **it**. Our space program has taken **its** place in the history of flight.

it's — contraction of **it is**. **It's** necessary to separate **it's** from **its**. (And remember that no such spelling as **its'** exists.)

it's

He wants to spend all his money, but _____ not a good idea.

its

The kitten played with the wool and got _____ paws all tangled.

15. **lead** — a heavy soft metal. Because **lead** is soft, it is malleable.

led — past tense of verb **to lead**. She **led** the horse to water and it drank.

led

He _____ a full life and died at 106.

lead

Many pipes are made of _____.

16. **lightening** — taking weight off. **Lightening** the load, he threw the parachutes out of the plane.

lightning — as in thunder and lightning. **Lightning** scares many small children.

Some unhappy people object to any

lightening

_____ of their burden of sorrows.

lightning

Thunder and _____ accompany many summer storms.

17. **precede, proceed** — see **-cede, -ceed, -sede** words at the end of this chapter.

18. **principal** — chief, important (*adjective*), director of a public school (*noun*). Our **principal** goal should be to clean up the environment.

principle — a rule or law (*noun*). An ancient **principle** of life is to do unto others as you would have them do unto you.

principal

His _____ goal is happiness.

principal

Ms. Smith is the _____ of our high school.

principles

His _____ were too high for the ordinary human being to follow.

19. **prophecy** — a prediction of things to come (*noun*). What is the astrologer's **prophecy** for today?

prophesy — to predict things to come (*verb*). Do you believe astrologers truly have the ability to **prophesy** the future?

prophesy

Computers now _____ the outcome of elections.

prophecy

One _____ for the future is that we will all be swamped in our own garbage.

20. **secede, succeed** — see **-cede, -ceed, -sede** words at the end of this chapter.

21. **their** — possessive pronoun. The girls said **their** goal was to go to Alaska.

there — present at that place. Put the book over **there.**

they're — contraction of **they are.** Many young boys say **they're** going to become football players.

they're

They said that _____ coming for the holidays.

their

They complained because _____ questions were left unanswered.

there

I want to climb Mt. Everest because it's _____.

22. **thorough** — complete, detailed, careful. We trusted him because his reports were always **thorough.**

though — even if, while. **Though** our heads are bloody, we remain unbowed.

thought — act of thinking (*noun*), past tense of **to think** (*verb*). He was so careless; he never gave his actions a **thought.**

threw — past tense of throw. She **threw** the ball over the roof.

through — many uses but most with the general meaning of passage from one side to another. He swam **through** the water with great ease.

threw

He _____ his coat on the floor instead of hanging it up.

I was happy to do it; don't give it another

thought   _____.

through   She walked _____ the woods.

thorough   The detective made a _____
                    investigation of the murder.

though   He smiled, _____ he was not very happy.

23. **to** — a preposition that usually shows movement
    towards something. He finally came **to** his senses.

    too — also, excessive. I'm going downtown; you
    come, **too.**

    two — the number 2. That hat cost **two** dollars.

two   If that hat cost _____ dollars, you were robbed.

to   Mary's coming ____ our house.

too   The pain was _____ great for her to bear.

24. **weather** — the condition of the atmosphere.
    Farmers think rain is good *weather*.

    whether — suggests alternatives. He didn't know
    whether to laugh or cry.

    The weather was so bad, she didn't know

whether   _____ to go or stay.

weather   We would grow bored if the _____ never
                     changed.

25. **were** — past tense of verb **to be.** We **were** going to
    go but changed our minds.

    we're — contraction of **we are.** You can stay home,
    but **we're** going.

    where — question regarding place. **Where** are we
    going anyway?

where   What I want to know is _____ are we now.

were   As a matter of fact, where _____ we yesterday?

we're   I can see _____ getting nowhere with this line
             of questioning.

26. **whose** — possessive of **who. Whose** little girl are you?

who's — contraction of **who is. Who's** your English teacher this term?

whose

I don't know _____ shoes they are.

Who's

_____ on first base?

27. **your** — possessive of **you.** Is she **your** little girl?

you're — contraction of **you are. You're** driving me crazy with that question.

You're

_____ taking a belligerent attitude.

your

I can't help it, _____ questions are driving me crazy.

-cede, -ceed, -sede

We might classify the words that end in the **seed** pronunciation as half sound-alikes. There are 12 such words, and they probably cause more trouble than they should. Let's take a look at them:

accede	exceed	recede
antecede	intercede	secede
cede	precede	succeed
concede	proceed	supersede

no

1. Do any of these words end in **s-e-e-d**? ____

Only the word **seed,** itself, is spelled **s-e-e-d.**

one

2. How many of the 12 words end in **s-e-d-e**? _____

Not too much memorization is required here. You need remember that only **supersede** has the s-e-d-e ending. You may remember more easily if you identify the **s** of **super** with the **s** of **sede.**

three

3. How many of the twelve words end in **c-e-e-d**? _____

exceed, proceed,

4. Which ones? _____

succeed

_____

58

A mnemonic sentence may help you keep these three together in your mind. **Proceed** with all due speed, but don't **exceed** the speed limit, or you'll only **succeed** in going to jail.

Now you can put the process of elimination to work for you. Remember **supersede, exceed, proceed,** and **succeed** are the outsiders in this group. Therefore any other words that end in the **seed** pronunciation are spelled **c-e-d-e.**

Now check yourself by filling in the blanks:

seceded

1. The southern states se_____d from the Union in 1860 and 1861.

intercede

2. Please inter_____ with my boss for me.

concede

3. The loser in an election usually con_____s to the winner.

precede

4. You go first; you pre_____ me through the door.

proceed

5. The parade will pro_____ along Fifth Avenue.

receded

6. The wave rushed up to the shore and then re_____d.

succeed

7. If at first you don't suc_____, try, try again.

cede

8. To give up title or ownership of land is to _____ the land.

accede

9. To agree with a point in an argument is to ac_____ to the point.

exceed

10. It's always tempting for people in power to ex_____ their power.

antecedes

11. While counting, **one** precedes **two;** that is, to put it another way, **one** ante_____s **two.**

superseded

12. After World War II, airplanes super_____d trains for long-distance travel.

(Circle all misspelled words in the passage below; then write the words correctly spelled into the numbered spaces provided. There may be more spaces provided than words misspelled. Finally, check your answers with the key that follows.)

The principle of our high school made a prophecy for our class. "You're not to bad a group," he said, "but there are some among you whose future does not look bright. Where they're going to end up is anybody's guess, but if they're no more through in their life's work than their school work, I have little hope of seeing them succeed. I conceed that I may be wrong about a few of them, but I haven't lead you this far to be dishonest now. But, for the hardworking members of the class, its' clear that you will be alright. I compliment you and urge you to go forward in life. My council to you is to chose a goal and march fearlessly to it."

Not everyone was altogether pleased with his speech.

1. _____   2. _____   3. _____

4. _____   5. _____   6. _____

7. _____   8. _____   9. _____

Key: Remember, in this group of words, you have to firmly connect the spelling of the word to its meaning. 1. *principal* 2. *too* 3. *thorough* 4. *concede* 5. *led* 6. *it's* 7. *all right* 8. *counsel* 9. *choose*

PART TWO
Visual-Centered Problems

8 Additive Elements

When you add a prefix, suffix, or word to another word or word part, do you know when to add letters, drop letters, or keep all of them? For example, when you add the suffix **-ness** to **drunken,** how do you spell the resulting combination — **drunke<u>n</u>ess** or **drunke<u>nn</u>ess**? And when you add the prefix **mis-** to **interpret,** is it **mi<u>s</u>interpret** or **mi<u>ss</u>interpret?**

This chapter, as others in this text, uses a special shortened form of programming. You could call it heuristic, but discovery programming is perhaps a better name. It's designed to ensure maximum involvement. You have to discover the rule governing additive elements. You're on the spot. As you can see, *you* have to get actively involved with this approach. That's why it works so well.

Actual classroom research compared the discovery-type unit which follows with a longer conventional programmed unit on the identical problem. The following 20-item unit was 5 percent more effective and took only 2½ minutes versus 8½ for the more conventional approach. So — take full advantage of this shortcut.

As you work through the following items, which contain no hyphenated combinations, what general rule can you discover? Once you discover the rule, you can spell literally thousands of troublesome words more easily. Even more important, since you discovered it yourself, you're not likely to forget it. And even if you do, you know how you arrived at it and can rediscover it anytime.

disservice	1. dis + service =	_____
reecho	2. dis + infect =	_____
disinfect		
reecho	3. re + echo =	_____
coordinal	4. co + ordinal =	_____
disagree	5. dis + agree =	_____

unnatural	6. un + natural =	_____
preempt	7. pre + empt =	_____
withhold	8. with + hold =	_____
newsstand	9. news + stand =	_____
overrun	10. over + run =	_____
thinness	11. thin + ness =	_____
disallow	12. dis + allow =	_____
unnerve	13. un + nerve =	_____
misstep	14. mis + step =	_____
interrelated	15. inter + related =	_____
shipment	16. ship + ment =	_____
outthink	17. out + think =	_____
solely	18. sole + ly =	_____
innovate	19. in + novate =	_____
knickknack	20. knick + knack =	_____

Now put down the rule you discovered: _____

_____

How close did you come to the phrasing given at the bottom of this page?*

To make the application of your newly discovered rule almost second nature, work through the next words in the same way.

professor	1. pro + fessor =	_____
reenter	2. re + enter =	_____
unneeded	3. un + needed =	_____

* When adding a prefix, suffix, or word to another word element, **retain all letters,** neither adding nor dropping any.

outtalk	4. out + talk =	_____
completely	5. complete + ly =	_____
unnoticed	6. un + noticed =	_____
dissatisfaction	7. dis + satisfaction =	_____
innumerable	8. in + numerable =	_____
overrate	9. over + rate =	_____
withholding	10. with + holding =	_____
interracial	11. inter + racial =	_____
coordinate	12. co + ordinate =	_____
disappoint	13. dis + appoint =	_____
cruelly	14. cruel + ly =	_____
preeminent	15. pre + eminent =	_____
disappear	16. dis + appear =	_____
disapprove	17. dis + approve =	_____
uncivilly	18. uncivil + ly =	_____
suddenness	19. sudden + ness =	_____
newssheet	20. news + sheet =	_____
coolly	21. cool + ly =	_____
finally	22. final + ly =	_____
incidentally	23. incidental + ly =	_____
really	24. real + ly =	_____
misspell	25. mis + spell =	_____

(Circle all misspelled words in the passage below; then write the word, correctly spelled, in the numbered spaces provided. There may be more spaces provided than words misspelled. Finally, check your answers with the key that follows.)

If your proffessor is dissatisfied with your innumerable

mispellings, focus more sharply on your troublemakers. Some

chapters in this book may actualy be slightly irrelevant or

unneeded. To make your spelling missteps dissappear more

rapidly, enter your own spelling demons on the pages in the

back of this text. Proofreading of this kind is a reminder that

your demons tend to go unoticed. It's unnatural to expect great

suddeness of improvement. Generaly speaking, however, if you

keep working, you'll finally realize that you have become a

really good speller.

1. _____   2. _____   3. _____

4. _____   5. _____   6. _____

7. _____   8. _____   9. _____

If you circled any other words except the ones listed, enter them on your personal spelling list in the back of this text.

Key: 1. professor 2. misspellings 3. actually 4. disappear 5. unnoticed 6. suddenness 7. generally

9 Final *e*

Now for another look at the final silent **e**. Since final silent **e**'s are found by the thousands, sprinkled through every page of your dictionary, that portion dealt with in Chapter 4 under vowel length is but a good beginning. Knowing the relationship between silent **e** and the vowel preceding it does help both in spelling and pronunciation, as you have discovered. It explains why **at** and **ate, Ed** and **cede, it** and **-ite, us** and **fuse** are all pronounced as they are. This in turn helps you pronounce and spell such relatively rare words as **alkane, rede,** or **fen.**

Another large group of words ending in silent **e** behaves in a special way when a suffix ending is added, a qualification of the principle dealt with in the chapter on additive elements. For example, which is the proper spelling — **desirable,** or **desireable**? The following exercises should help you with all such problems.

1. Notice that final silent **e** is generally dropped before a suffix beginning with a vowel but retained before a

consonant

suffix beginning with a _____, as in **care, caring,** and **careful.**

hoping (suffix begins with vowel) hopeless (suffix begins with consonant)

2. That means that when you add **-ing** and **-less** to **hope,** you get _____ g and _____ s.

3. And when you add **-ing** to **argue,** you add a suffix beginning with a vowel, so you should spell the

arguing

resulting combination _____.

4. And when you add **-ed** to **argue,** that suffix also begins with a vowel so you should drop the final silent **e** and spell the resulting combination

argued

_____.

67

5. But with words ending in **ue,** as **argue, due,** and
   true, the final **e** is also dropped before a suffix
   beginning with a consonant, as in **argue + ment,**
   spelled **argument, due + ly,** spelled **duly,** and

truly

   true + ly, spelled _____.

6. Words containing a **c** or **g** just before the silent **e**
   make up another special group, as with which two

   words — **notice, excuse,** or **courage?**_____

notice / courage

   _____.

7. When the **c** has the **s** sound and the **g** a **j** sound, the
   silent **e** is kept before the two suffixes — **-able** and
   -ous. Notice + able would, by this subrule, be

noticeable

   spelled _____.

8. When you add **-ous** to **courage,** since the **g** has a **j**
   sound, and **-ous** is one of the two suffixes where the
   subrule applies, you should spell the combination

courageous

   _____.

9. These special spellings apply only with **-able** and
   -ous. Notice + able is, therefore, **noticeable,** but

noticing

   notice + ing would be spelled _____.

10. Add **-able** to **replace.** Since the **c** has the sound of **s,**

replaceable

    you spell the combination _____.

replacing

11. Add **-ing** to **replace** and you have _____,
    since the suffix is neither **-able** nor **-ous.**

traceable
tracing

12. Add **-able** and **-ing** to **trace** and you get
    _____ able and _____ing.

changeable
changed

13. Add **-able** and **-ed** to **change** and you get
    _____ and _____.

68

14. Now see if you can manage all these combinations correctly. They review a very important rule:

ninety   **nine + -ty =**   _____

valuable   **value + -able =**   _____

manageable   **manage + -able =**   _____

duly   **due + -ly =**   _____

charging   **charge + -ing =**   _____

advisable   **advise + -able =**   _____

15. To summarize, with words ending in a final silent **e**, drop the **e** before a suffix beginning with a

vowel   _____ .

16. With words containing a **c** or **g** before the silent **e**,

_s_

when the **c** has the sound of _____ and the **g** the

_j_

sound of _____, that final silent **e** is retained with the suffixes **-able** and **-ous**.

Other exceptions, and there are quite a few because the silent **e** ending is so common, are best memorized individually if they pose difficulties for you. Add them to your personal list in the back.

To ensure increased accuracy in the application of these principles, including the most common exceptions, work thoughtfully through the following items. Whenever you miss one, check the rule again.

Exercise 1

Write the proper spelling of the following combinations:

losing   1. lose + ing =   _____

careless   2. care + less =   _____

chosen   3. chose + en =   _____

receivable   4. receive + able =   _____

safety   5. safe + ty =   _____

conceivable   6. conceive + able =   _____

writing   7. write + ing =   _____

argument   8. argue + ment =   _____

accommodation   9. accommodate + ion =   _____

improvement   10. improve + ment =   _____

mileage   11. mile + age =   _____

truly   12. true + ly =   _____

desirable   13. desire + able =   _____

commencement   14. commence + ment =   _____

nervous   15. nerve + ous =   _____

crippling   16. cripple + ing =   _____

imaginary   17. imagine + ary =   _____

sensible   18. sense + ible =   _____

judgment   19. judge + ment =   _____

assemblage   20. assemble + age =   _____

hoeing   21. hoe + ing =   _____

coming   22. come + ing =   _____

arrangement   23. arrange + ment =   _____

management   24. manage + ment =   _____

fiercely   25. fierce + ly =   _____

Exercise 2

Write the proper spelling of the following combinations:

advantageous	1. advantage + ous =	_____
pursuable	2. pursue + able =	_____
decided	3. decide + ed =	_____
forcibly	4. forcible + ly =	_____
noticeable	5. notice + able =	_____
lodgment	6. lodge + ment =	_____
immediately	7. immediate + ly =	_____
ninety	8. nine + ty =	_____
careful	9. care + ful =	_____
achieved	10. achieve + ed =	_____
changeable	11. change + able =	_____
practical	12. practice + al =	_____
courageous	13. courage + ous =	_____
marriageable	14. marriage + able =	_____
fascinating	15. fascinate + ing =	_____
duly	16. due + ly =	_____
merely	17. mere + ly =	_____
preceding	18. precede + ing =	_____
purchasable	19. purchase + able =	_____
useful	20. use + ful =	_____
livable	21. live + able =	_____

prejudiced	22. prejudice + ed =	_____
definitely	23. definite + ly =	_____
believes	24. believe + s =	_____
exaggerated	25. exaggerate + ed =	_____

PROOFREADING EXERCISE

(Circle all misspelled words in the passage below; then write the words, correctly spelled, in the numbered spaces provided. There may be more spaces provided than words misspelled. Finally, check your answers with the key that follows.)

It's definitly advantageous to remember your diagnostic test scores, especially those areas of major difficulty. Improvement there will be most noticable. Use careful judgment in the useful arrangement of your study activities. Be truely sensible in planning desireable study times. Remember — no spelling problem is hopeless. You can make any problem more managable.

1. _____   2. _____   3. _____

4. _____   5. _____   6. _____

Key: 1. definitely 2. noticeable 3. truly 4. desirable 5. manageable

10 Assimilative Changes

Perhaps the single principle of most help in understanding the makeup of countless English words, both their spelling and meaning, is the principle called "assimilation." Using this principle, you can usually reason out for yourself the probable correct spelling of a whole host of troublemakers. For example, which is correct — **professor** or **proffessor, occurrence** or **ocurrence, inoculate** or **innoculate**? As you can see, the principle of assimilation governs that part of a word where prefix joins root or stem.

What's assimilation? For an answer, work through the following exercises.

consonant

1. The following prefixes — **ad-, com-, dis-, ex-, in-, ob-,** and **sub-** are alike in that they all end in a single final (vowel / consonant).

one

2. These prefixes are alike also in that they all have _____ syllable, not two.

sub-

3. Assimilative change ordinarily occurs only with prefixes of one syllable, ending in a consonant, such as (**re- / inter- / sub-**).

d

4. Add the Latin prefix **ad-** (meaning "to" or "toward") to **ply** and you get **adply.** Now pronounce that combination slowly, then rapidly. What letter sound tends to disappear — the sound of **d** or **p**?

apply

5. This explains why, when you add **ad-** to **ply,** you spell the resulting combination _____, not **adply.**

p

6. This is called an assimilative change because the **d** of **ad** is absorbed or assimilated by the **p** to become _____, not **d.**

7. The word **assimilate** both names and illustrates this change. Pronounce **adsimilate** slowly, then faster. What letter sound tends to disappear? The sound of

d _____.

8. When one letter is assimilated by another, it becomes

similar like or s_____ to the other.

9. That is why the change is called assimilation or

assimilative _____tive doubling or change.

10. Assimilative changes provide a more easily pronounced combination. Take **dis** + **ficult.** Which is

difficult easier to say — **disficult** or **difficult**?

11. Now for help with your spelling, see if the word in
question contains a prefix which ordinarily under-
goes assimilation. Say the word, using the common

assimilated form of the prefix, then with the _____ed
form. See which is easier to say.

12. For example, is it **acept** or **accept**? If the word contains the prefix **ad-,** pronounce **adcept** and **accept**

accept distinctly. Which is easier?

13. When **ad-** is placed before **fect,** which is easier to

affect pronounce — **adfect** or **affect**?

14. When you add **ad-** to **cidental,** you have reason to

accidental spell the resulting word _____.

15. When you add **ad-** to **commodate,** you get

accommodate _____.

16. And the word **append** is but a combination of **ad-**
and **pend,** so you spell it by changing the first **d** to

p _____.

17. Noting the prefix meaning will usually help you determine the presence of a prefix. For example, is it

74

attend

attend or **atend?** Since **ad-** means "to," you look for the idea of "to" in the word. When you go **to** class, you at_____.

appropriate

18. If something is relevant **to** a situation, we say it is what — **adpropriate, apropriate,** or **appropriate?**

aggressive

19. When you make progress, you move ahead. When you move **to** or **toward,** as in a battle, your action is what — **adgressive, agressive,** or **aggressive?**

annex

20. A building which is added **to** another is called what — **adnex, anex,** or **annex?**

approach

21. Which of these words probably has an assimilated form of the prefix **ad-**: **athlete** or **approach?**

address

22. You don't **red**ress a letter to get it **to** the right person. You _____dress it.

consonant

23. The sign of a pawnshop is three golden balls. Similarly, the visual sign of assimilation is a doubled _____sonant, where prefix joins root.

At this point, check up on your assimilative know-how, using the following discovery-type exercises. Combine the prefix and root elements given below into the correct spelling. Whenever you miss a word recheck and rethink to ensure improved performance with the thousands of words governed by this principle. Keep the answers covered until you're ready to check.

eccentric	1. ex + centric =	_____
inoculate	2. in + oculate =	_____
irrigate	3. in + rigate =	_____
offer	4. ob + fer =	_____
irresistible	5. in + resistible =	_____
arrange	6. ad + range =	_____

professor	7. pro + fessor =	_____
immigrate	8. in + migrate =	_____
recommend	9. re + commend =	_____
occupy	10. ob + cupy =	_____
attract	11. ad + tract =	_____
differ	12. dis + fer =	_____
assumption	13. ad + sumption =	_____
among	14. a + mong =	_____
irregular	15. in + regular =	_____
colleague	16. com + league =	_____
appear	17. ad + pear =	_____
different	18. dis + ferent =	_____
resemble	19. re + semble =	_____
illegible	20. in + legible =	_____
annexation	21. ad + nexation =	_____
procedure	22. pro + cedure =	_____
opposition	23. ob + position =	_____
support	24. sub + port =	_____
assemble	25. ad + semble =	_____

Normally, of course, when you spell a word you're not given the prefix and root parts. You must analyze the word yourself to see if it contains a prefix. When you've identified the probable prefix, you're in a position to know whether to expect assimilative change or not.

Fortunately, about 90 percent of all assimilative changes occur with only seven prefixes. If you know them and their common meaning, you can handle assimilative changes more easily.

Here are the changeable prefixes, together with their most common meanings:

(1) **ad-** means to (or toward)

(2) **com-** means together (or with)

(3) **dis-** means apart (or away)

(4) **ex-** means out (or formerly)

(5) **in-** means not or in

(6) **ob-** means against (or toward)

(7) **sub-** means under

In analyzing words, lean both on prefix form and prefix meaning. For example, which is correct — **anotate** or **annotate**?

Put analysis to work. Since the word begins with **a**, and only one of the seven prefixes begins with that letter, check the word meaning to see if it reflects the meaning "to." When you add notes **to** something, you do what — **anotate** or **annotate**? The meaning **to** suggests the prefix **ad-** and the double **n** spelling of normal assimilative change.

For added experience, try the exercise that follows. Cover the three answer columns to the left before you begin. Look at the absurd phonetic-type spellings and try to figure out exactly what words are intended. Then write the correct spelling of the word in Column I, the probable prefix contained in the word in Column II, and the prefix meaning in Column III. Feel free to check back on prefix meaning if you're not sure. Then uncover the three columns of answers, check and go on to the next word. You'll develop enviable know-how in this way.

Assimilative Changes

	Column I Probable Spelling	Column II Probable Prefix	Column III Prefix Meaning
1. **kuhNEKT** the wires	_____	_____	_____
2. **suhPRES** the uprising	_____	_____	_____
3. an **iMEZHyurble** distance	_____	_____	_____
4. the **iMEEdeeut** future	_____	_____	_____
5. to attend **CAWlij**	_____	_____	_____
6. recording **apuhRATus**	_____	_____	_____
7. **earASHunl** behavior	_____	_____	_____
8. her **efYOOsiv** manner	_____	_____	_____
9. **KUMing** over the hill	_____	_____	_____

Answers for

Column I	Column II	Column III
connect	com-	together
suppress	sub-	under
immeasurable	in-	not
immediate	in-	in
college	com-	together
apparatus	ad-	to
irrational	in-	not
effusive	ex-	out
coming	none	

	Column I Probable Spelling	Column II Probable Prefix	Column III Prefix Meaning
10. **kuMITee** report			
11. a bad **kuhLIZHun**			
12. **ahFENsiv** action			
13. newly **ALokated**			
14. with great **EFurt**			
15. an **iLITerut** man			
16. **ahPOZing** team			
17. **aKOMadate** the change			
18. the gas **difYOOZD**			
19. music **aFEKTS** him			
20. **suhKUM** to pressure			

Column I	Column II	Column III
committee	com-	together
collision	com-	together
offensive	ob-	against
allocated	ad-	to
effort	ex-	out
illiterate	in-	not.
opposing	ob-	against
accommodate	ad-	to
diffused	dis-	away
affects	ad-	to
succumb	sub-	under

Now let's see how far you've come. Think back to the opening paragraph of this chapter. Is it **professor** or **proffessor**? Reason it out. You know that **pro-** isn't one of the seven changeable prefixes. Furthermore, you can't think of a single English word beginning with **ff.** Even the dictionary won't supply one. That gives you two reasons for saying **professor** is the correct spelling.

And what about **occurrence** and **ocurrence**? Reason that out also. You know the root is **cur**, as in **recur, incur,** and the like. What's the only prefix beginning with **o** on the list? Why **ob-**, of course. It's not easy to pronounce **obcurrence**, so assimilation seems natural. That's the case for the correct spelling — **occurrence.**

Finally, is it **inoculation** or **innoculation?** Just ask yourself if the root is **ocu** or **nocu.** Since you can probably think of more words beginning with **ocu**, such as **oculist** and **ocular,** than words beginning with **nocu,** you have reason to suppose this word is a combination of **in-** and **ocu.** It should be spelled **inoculate.** The background you've been developing lets you reason your way through most of the spelling problems dealt with in this chapter. To be sure, there are exceptions — with this rule as with others. But don't worry. You know what words give you problems — what words give you mental blocks. Those are the ones to put into your personal list of demons. Review them from time to time. Make up mnemonics to help. Use the writing-saying-hearing-tracing technique.* And eventually they're no longer spelling problems. You've conquered them.

* Look ahead to Chapter 14 for further explanation of these techniques.

PROOFREADING EXERCISE

(Circle all misspelled words in the passage below; then write the words, correctly spelled, in the numbered spaces provided. There may be more spaces provided than words misspelled. Finally, check your answers with the key that follows.)

How are you comming along? Take this opportunity to address

yourself to the task of spotting diferent examples of asimilative

change. How many apparent ocurrences appear? Irational effort

won't help you assemble them. Accept the challenge. Find all

the iregular spellings. Knowledge of this principle can have an

imeasureable effect on your spelling.

1. _____ 2. _____ 3. _____

4. _____ 5. _____ 6. _____

7. _____ 8. _____ 9. _____

Key: 1. coming 2. different 3. assimilative 4. occurrences 5. irrational 6. irregular 7. immeasurable

11 **Plurals**

If you are willing to learn a few rules, the mastery of forming plurals should come fairly easily for you. The overwhelming majority of English words are made plural simply by adding the letter **s.** Thus: **bed, beds; book, books; pen, pens; song, songs; telephone, telephones;** and so forth. But, English being English there are exceptions to this rule. Most of the exceptions are easily identified and for the most part easily handled.

The exceptions for which you must learn some rules are words that end in **y, o,** and **f;** words that end in a sibilant such as **church, thrush, lass, tax,** and **buzz;** some nouns borrowed from foreign languages that have retained their foreign plurals; some irregular English nouns; and compound nouns such as **brother-in-law.**

Words that end in *y*

The alphabet is divided into vowels (**a, e, i, o, u,** sometimes **y**) and consonants (any letter not a vowel). With this fact in mind, examine the following list of words that end in **y** and their plural forms shown in the second column. Be alert to whether a vowel or a consonant precedes the **y** in the singular form of the word.

activity	activities
apology	apologies
duty ˙	duties
attorney	attorneys
monkey	monkeys
toy	toys

consonant, y

1. In the first three singular words of the list a _____ precedes the final __.

vowel

y

2. In the last three singular words of the list a_____ precedes the final __.

3. For the singular words where the final **y** is preceded by

i

es

a vowel, the plural is formed by changing final **y** to ___ and adding ___.

4. For the singular words where the final **y** is preceded by

s

y

a vowel, the plural is formed by simply adding ___ to the final ___.

Good, you now know almost all you need to know about forming the plural of words that end in **y.** Try your hand at writing the rules for yourself.

- Words that end in a consonant plus **y** are pluralized by

_____

Answer: changing the final **y** to **i** and adding **es.**

- Words that end in a vowel plus *y* are pluralized by

_____

Answer: simply adding **s** to the final **y.**

Now try your hand at forming a few plurals from words that end in **y.**

puppies   1. puppy   _____

chimneys   2. chimney   _____

plays   3. play   _____

days   4. day   _____

bodies   5. body   _____

studies   6. study   _____

boys   7. boy   _____

libraries   8. library   _____

If you missed none of the words on the list, you have mastered the rules that govern words that end in **y.** If you missed any words, work your way through the sequence again.

Now you are ready for an exception to the rule. (You knew there would be one, didn't you?) Proper nouns such as people's names retain the integrity of their spelling in plural form. Therefore, last names such as **Berry** and **Kelly** simply add an **s** to form their plurals and become **Berrys** and **Kellys.**

Words that end in *o*

Words that end in an **o** preceded by a vowel present no particular problem. Examine the following list:

boo	boos
curio	curios
radio	radios
rodeo	rodeos
studio	studios

vowel   1. In each word the final **o** is preceded by a _____.

s   2. For each word the plural is formed by adding an __.

o   3. Complete the rule: Words that end in an __

vowel   preceded by a _____ are pluralized by adding

s   an __.

Words that end in an **o** preceded by a vowel, then, present no problem to you. They are pluralized by simply adding an **s** in the normal way of most English words. Fix the rule in your mind and spell such words with confidence.

Words that end in a consonant plus **o** are a different matter entirely. They are not nearly as simple to live with. Examine the following list:

banjo	banjos
cargo	cargoes
echo	echoes
hero	heroes
piano	pianos
tomato	tomatoes
zero	zeros

o   1. All the words on the list end in an __ preceded by a

consonant   _____.

2. The words **banjo, piano,** and **zero** form their plur-

s

als by adding ___.

3. The words **cargo, echo, hero,** and **tomato** form

es

their plurals by adding ___.

Obviously, then, in words ending in consonant plus **o,** you have no simple rule to guide you. Some form their plurals by adding an **s** and some with **es.** For these words you must either memorize them or, like most of us, depend upon your dictionary when you must spell them. One tip may help you a little. Musical terms that end in **o** usually form their plurals by simply adding an **s.** Examine the following list:

alto	altos	contralto	contraltos
banjo	banjos	piano	pianos
basso	bassos	solo	solos
concerto	concertos	soprano	sopranos

● All are musical terms and all form their plurals by

s

adding ___.

Now test yourself on the following list. If need be, consult your dictionary for words that end in consonant plus **o.**

cameos   1. cameo   _____

cantos   2. canto   _____

dittos   3. ditto   _____

embargoes   4. embargo   _____

frescoes or frescos   5. fresco   _____

gigolos   6. gigolo   _____

mementos   7. memento   _____

patios   8. patio   _____

piccolos   9. piccolo   _____

pintos   10. pinto   _____

potatoes	11. potato	_____
ratios	12. ratio	_____
silos	13. silo	_____
stereos	14. stereo	_____
taboos	15. taboo	_____
tomatoes	16. tomato	_____
tornadoes or tornados	17. tornado	_____
volcanos	18. volcano	_____

You should have had no trouble with the words that end with a vowel plus **o,** or the two musical terms, **canto** and **piccolo.** The other words you would have had either to know already or to find in your dictionary. Note that for some words like **fresco** and **tornado** either plural form is correct. Dictionaries sometimes list such alternative spellings of plurals.

Words that end in *f*

Words that end in **f** may or may not be a problem to you when forming plurals. If your ear is good and you pronounce words well, you know that some words ending in **f** change the pronunciation of their roots in the plural and some do not. For example, **leaf** becomes **leaves** but **roof** becomes **roofs.** The changing of the **f** to **ve** and the adding of the **s** is heard clearly in the pronunciation.

Test yourself on the following words. Say their plurals aloud and then write the plural.

beliefs	1. belief	_____
chiefs	2. chief	_____
lives	3. life	_____
loaves	4. loaf (as in loaf of bread)	_____

mischiefs	5. mischief	_____
scarfs or scarves	6. scarf	_____
selves	7. self	_____
sheriffs	8. sheriff	_____
tariffs	9. tariff	_____
wives	10. wife	_____

If you correctly spelled the ten words on the list, you can probably spell most words that end in **f** with confidence. You have a good ear. If you misspelled several of them, you are going to have to depend upon your dictionary when you form plurals for words that end in **f**. As you use the dictionary, pronounce the word correctly as well as spelling it correctly. In time your pronunciation should become a proper guide to the most common of our words that end in **f**. One tip that may help: most words that end in double **f**, such as **sheriff**, form their plurals simply by adding **s** without a root change.

Words that end in a sibilant

Words that end in a sibilant (**ch, sh, s, x, z**) present no great problem. Examine the following list, saying both the singular and plural forms aloud.

boss	bosses
box	boxes
bush	bushes
buzz	buzzes
catch	catches

es   1. In each case the plural is formed by adding ____.

        2. When you have pronounced the plural aloud, you should have noticed that adding the **es** also added an

syllable   extra _____.

Good. Now write a rule to cover the forming of plurals for words that end in a sibilant.

88

● Words that end in a sibilant _____

_____

Answer: form their plurals by adding **es**. The **es** is pronounced as an added syllable.

Test yourself by forming the plurals of the following words. Some of the words in the test list do not end in a sibilant and, therefore, do not add an **es**. Say the words aloud, listening for the sibilant sound in the singular form and the added syllable in the plural.

bashes	1. bash	_____
cars	2. car	_____
dresses	3. dress	_____
foxes	4. fox	_____
windows	5. window	_____
klutzes	6. klutz	_____
cabinets	7. cabinet	_____
papers	8. paper	_____
latches	9. latch	_____

Foreign borrowings

Some of the words we have borrowed from foreign languages have retained their original plural endings. Others of these are now correct with either the original foreign plural or with a conventional **s** or **es** ending. Here is a very partial list consisting of words commonly enough used that they are probably worth memorizing:

agendum	agenda
analysis	analyses
appendix	appendices or appendixes
crisis	crises
criterion	criteria
datum	data

formula	formulae or formulas
focus	foci or focuses
hypothesis	hypotheses
thesis	theses
vertebra	vertebrae or vertebras

Irregular English plurals

In addition to the plurals that are irregular because they are borrowed from a foreign language, we have numerous nouns of English origin that do not form their plurals in the regular way. Chances are that you already know most of the common ones. Here is a representative list:

child	children	mouse	mice
deer	deer	ox	oxen
foot	feet	sheep	sheep
goose	geese	swine	swine
man	men	tooth	teeth
moose	moose	woman	women

Compound nouns

Generally speaking, compound nouns form their plurals by adding a conventional **s** or **es** ending to the main word in the compound as in this list:

attorney at law	attorneys at law
brigadier general	brigadier generals
brother-in-law	brothers-in-law
consul general	consuls general
passer-by	passers-by

Sometimes the trick is to decide which word of the compound is the main word. As always, if in doubt consult your dictionary.

Third person singular of the verb

Verbs in the present tense generally have an **s** or **es** added to them when they are formed into the third person singular. Thus it would be **I see, you see, we see,** and **they see,** but **he, she, or it sees.** When the verb is used in the third person singular and needs **es** or **s** added to it, you can usually apply the same rules you have learned for pluralizing nouns.

PROOFREADING EXERCISE

(Circle all misspelled words in the passage below; then write the words correctly spelled into the numbered spaces provided. There may be more spaces provided than words misspelled. Finally, check your answers with the key that follows.)

"I make no apologys for my attorneys," said famous person Cassie Tilly, of the Virginia Tillies. "Their job was to prove that my late husband had intended to leave his estate to me and not to my two sister-in-laws or his three previous wifes. In a case so difficult, there were no ready formulas they could follow. They had to be regular foxes, and they were."

She smiled a satisfied smile as she settled one of her mink scarves about her shoulders. "I have only one criteria in my life," she said. "If you can't eat it, drink it, wear it, or spend it, why bother? Right?" As she talked, she gave out to passer-bys a list of the possessions in her late husband's estate. The list included such items as four boxs of jewels, three stereoes, two grand pianos, and one basso in a pear tree.

1. _____ 2. _____ 3. _____

4. _____ 5. _____ 6. _____

7. _____ 8. _____ 9. _____

Key: 1. apologies: a consonant preceding a y, use ies 2. Tillys: remember proper nouns keep the integrity of their spelling in the plural 3. sisters-in-law: pluralize the main word in compounds 4. wives: say wife/wives 5. criterion is the singular form, criteria the plural 6. passers-by: passer is the main word 7. boxes: hear the added syllable 8. stereos: o preceded by a vowel takes only an s

12 **The Hyphen**

One of the trickier marks of punctuation that play a role in spelling is the hyphen. The use of the hyphen in spelling falls into three categories: (1) common compound words, (2) compounds used as adjectives, and (3) numbers and fractions.

Common compound words

Common compound words are words that are used together often enough that they have come to be considered as fixed compounds. Therefore, they will be found in most dictionaries. The following compound words are all written here as two words. Actually some should be written as one word, some as a hyphenated word, and some as you see them, two words.

In the first blank after each compound, spell the word as you think it should be. Then check the spelling in your dictionary. If the dictionary's spelling is different from yours, put it in the second place.

color bearer   _____   _____

color blind   _____   _____

color guard   _____   _____

glass house   _____   _____

house party   _____   _____

house raising   _____   _____

house wife   _____   _____

red head   _____   _____

red letter   _____   _____

red light   _____   _____

school board	_____	_____
self expression	_____	_____
self hood	_____	_____
self identity	_____	_____
self made	_____	_____
self same	_____	_____
text book	_____	_____
wrist band	_____	_____

Almost certainly when you checked your dictionary you found that you had numerous misspellings. The truth of the matter is that few rules apply that will help you decide whether a common compound should be written as one word, a hyphenated word, or two words. When such chaos exists, only one rule can pertain: if you are using a common compound word in a document in which correctness is important, such as a job application, a business letter, or a school essay, check the word in your dictionary. The dictionary we checked (*Webster's Third New International Dictionary*) spelled the words above as follows: **color-bearer, color-blind, color guard,** **glasshouse, house party, house-raising, housewife, redhead, red-letter, red light, school board, self-expression, self-identity, selfhood, self-made, selfsame, textbook,** and **wristband.**

You may find — such is the chaos in this matter — that your dictionary and ours do not agree on all the words. Accept both this fact and the spelling that your dictionary gives.

Compounds as adjectives

We are on a little firmer ground when we consider compound words used as adjectives. Some compound adjectives — like **red-letter, self-made,** and **selfsame** — are common compounds and can be found in the dictionary. But many others are simply compounds that we ourselves create to modify nouns that we use. We may wish to write, for example, of a **foreign car salesperson.** In such an expression we have an obvious chance for misunderstanding. Is it the **car** or the **salesperson** that is foreign? Correct punctuation clears up the ambiguity. In the expression **a foreign, car salesperson,** the salesperson is foreign. If you write the expression as **a foreign-car salesperson,** then the car is foreign. It makes a big difference to the rabbit whether it is a **pink, skinned rabbit** or a **pink-skinned rabbit.**

Generally speaking, when we compound words and use them as adjectives **before** the noun modified, we hyphenate them. Look at the following:

> the **six-cylinder** engine
> Their **too-little-and-too-late** methods
> a **slow-flying** airplane
> the **pay-as-you-go** tax plan
> a **six-year** prison sentence
> a **health-related** issue
> his **up-to-date** methods

Now examine this list. Note the absence of hyphens and also the absence of ambiguity:

> The airplane is **slow flying.**
> The tax plan calls for you to **pay as you go.**
> The issue was **health related.**
> His methods are **up to date.**

From your observations, form a rule that will guide you in forming most compound adjectives.

• When compounds are used as adjectives _____

_____

_____

_____

Answer: and are placed before the noun modified, to avoid ambiguity, they are commonly hyphenated. When the compound appears after the noun, the meaning is usually clear and, therefore, the compound is generally not hyphenated.

Numbers and fractions

Examine the following list of numbers written as words. Note how they are hyphenated or not hyphenated:

nine	twenty	sixty-six
ten	twenty-three	eighty-six

fourteen	twenty-five	ninety-nine
sixteen	sixty	one hundred and ninety-nine

From your observations, form a rule that will guide you in hyphenating numbers.

- _____

_____

_____

Answer: When numbers are written as words, numbers from twenty through ninety-nine that are compound numbers such as twenty-four and seventy-six are hyphenated.

Write the following numbers as words:

fourteen	14	_____
thirty-seven	37	_____
forty-nine	49	_____
sixteen	16	_____
fifty-two	52	_____
one hundred and thirty-two	132	_____

Examine the following list of fractions written as words. Note how they are hyphenated:

one-half	four thirty-seconds
three-eighths	twenty-two fourths
four-fifths	five one-hundredths
four-ninths	thirty-three thirds

Paying particular attention to the numerators and denominators, form a rule from the above list that will guide you in hyphenating fractions written as words.

- _____

  _____

  _____

Answer: Normally, place a hyphen between the numerator and denominator of fractions written as words. However, when either the numerator or denominator is already hyphenated, omit the hyphen between the two.

Write the following fractions as words:

one-eighth	1/8	_____
two-ninths	2/9	_____
five-sixths	5/6	_____
forty-four ninths	44/9	_____
three ten-thousandths	3/10,000	_____
nine-tenths	9/10	_____

A good dictionary and the rules you have worked out in this chapter will serve you for most of the normal hyphenation problems you are likely to run into in school work and business correspondence. Should you have problems beyond the ordinary, such as, for instance, you might have in writing or editing scientific papers, we recommend you to *The Chicago Manual of Style.*

(Circle all misspelled words in the passage below; then write the words correctly spelled into the numbered spaces provided. There may be more spaces provided than words misspelled. Finally, check your answers with the key that follows.)

John had just turned twentyone, and he had never been happier. The day he had turned eighteen had been a red letter day he thought. His much-loved grand father had given him a used car for a present. John had that day folded his six-foot frame into the car's front seat and driven all around town with a devil may care attitude. But, today was different. Now he was independent, on his own. While putting his check book in his pocket, he glanced at the balance in his account. It was lower than he would have liked. He had already spent one half his week's pay, and it was only Monday. Being independent did have its head aches. Should he borrow money from his family, he wondered. His self-less mother would give him some, he knew. He decided not to. He wanted to be a selfreliant man. Feeling better with this self-confident decision, John whistled happily and left his apartment to visit his stay-at-home girl friend, Mary.

1. _____   2. _____   3. _____

4. _____   5. _____   6. _____

7. _____   8. _____   9. _____

Key: 1. *twenty-one:* compound numbers between twenty and ninety-nine written as words are hyphenated 2. *red-letter:* check your dictionary 3. *grandfather:* check your dictionary 4. *devil-may-care:* Compound adjectives before the noun are normally hyphenated 5. *checkbook:* check your dictionary 6. *one-half:* fractions written as words are normally hyphenated 7. *headaches:* check your dictionary 8. *selfless:* check your dictionary 9. *self-reliant:* check your dictionary

13 Apostrophes

The apostrophe is used to form the possessive case, to replace omitted letters and numbers, and to make plurals of letters and numbers. Let's examine each of these uses.

Possessive case

Our explanations on how to form the possessive case follow those found in *The Chicago Manual of Style*. All style guides agree on the general principles involved, but a few disagree on some of the details. We have chosen to follow *The Chicago Manual* because of its wide acceptance as a guide, and because its rules strike us as eminently sensible and practical.

Read each example sentence in Groups A, B, C, D, E, and F, which follow. Pay close attention to the words in boldface type. Work the exercises that follow the examples. Remember to keep covered the answers that appear on the left.

Group A: Possessive of singular words.

(1) He dropped the **girl's hat.**
(2) **Charles's book** was lost.
(3) The **wind's velocity** was twenty miles per hour.
(4) The **father's permission** for the wedding was given.
(5) The **President's signing** of the bill made it law.
(6) Although he was forty-six, he lived in a **boy's world.**

apostrophe

1. What mark of punctuation do the first words in every boldface group have in common?_____

s

2. What letter follows each apostrophe? __

3. In each sentence does the person or thing represented by the first boldface word possess in some way the object or action represented by the second boldface word?

yes

_____

99

Fill in the two blanks to complete the rule:

apostrophe, s

- Singular words are formed into the possessive case by adding an _____ and the letter __.

In the phrases below fill in the blanks properly to form the possessive case:

Jack's

1. Jack_____ coat

Marx's

2. Marx_____ principles

hurricane's

3. the hurricane_____ force

team's

4. the team_____ winning

In your own words state the rule for forming singular words into the possessive case:

- _____

_____

Answer: Singular words are made possessive by adding an apostrophe and the letter s.

There are a few exceptions to the above rule. When adding an apostrophe and an **s** results in an extra, awkward **s** or **z** sound, only the apostrophe is used. The words chiefly affected are words like **appearance, conscience,** and **righteousness,** the names **Jesus** and **Moses,** and ancient proper names that end in an **eez** sound, such as **Euripides.** To see the reason for this rule compare the ease of saying **Moses' staff** with the difficulty of **Moses's staff.** For another comparison, notice that **Charles's book** or **Marx's principles** present no difficulty and, therefore, are written in the normal manner with an apostrophe and an **s.**

Try your hand with these examples:

Jesus'

1. Jesus__ shroud

jazz's

2. jazz__ power

Bob's

3. Bob__ horse

Xerxes'

4. Xerxes__ sword

Demosthenes'   5. Demosthenes__ pebbles

man's   6. the man__ pencil

righteousness'   7. in righteousness__ way

James's   8. James__ room

Group B: Possessive of plural words

(1) He looked into the three **horses' mouths.**
(2) The **spectators' scrambling** for seats caused a fight.
(3) The **children's coats** were torn.
(4) The **men's eyes** filled with tears.

Fill in the blanks to complete the rule:

s
apostrophe

apostrophe
s

• Plural words that end in the letter __ are made possessive by adding an _____ only.
Irregular plural words that do not end in an **s** are made plural by adding an _____ and an __.

In the phrases below fill in the blanks properly to form the possessive case:

cats'   1. the six cat__ pajamas

media's   2. the media__ rights to free speech

oxen's   3. the oxen__ yokes

attorneys'   4. the three attorney__ cases

In your own words state the rule for forming plural words into the possessive case:

• _____

_____

_____

Answer: When plural words end in **s**, form the possessive case by adding an apostrophe only. When plural words do not end in **s**, add an apostrophe and an **s**.

In the following phrases there are both singular and plural situations. Form the possessives by filling in the blanks properly:

Moses'   1. Moses____ cradle

desk's   2. the desk____ top

players'   3. the players____ intensity

appearance'   4. for appearance____ sake

Euripides'   5. Euripides____ tragedies

night's   6. a night____ work

governor's   7. the governor____ passing

children's   8. the children____ shouts

Group C: Possessive of compound nouns.

(1) My **father-in-law's barn** burned down.
(2) **Henry VIII's eating habits** were messy.
(3) The **executive directors' orders** confused everyone.

1. Phrases such as **father-in-law, executive director, associate professor,** and so forth are compound nouns. The phrase **Elizabeth II** is

compound   a _____ noun.

2. Examine the compound nouns in Group C. Are they

yes   in the possessive case? _____

3. In the case of compound nouns, where is the apostrophe plus **s** or the apostrophe alone added?

_____

Answer: At the end of the element closest to the thing possessed.

102

In the phrases below fill in the blanks properly to form the possessive case.

sister-in-law's   1. My sister-in-law_____ car

John J. Jones III's   2. John J. Jones III_____ blue Cadillac

the three vice   3. the three vice presidents_____ executive bathroom
presidents'

In your own words state the rule for forming the possessive for compound
nouns:

● _____

  _____

  _____

Answer: Compound nouns form the possessive by adding either apostrophe plus s or the apostrophe alone to the part of the compound closest to the thing possessed.

Group D: Possessive of coordinate nouns

(1) **Anne and Henry's experiment** blew up the laboratory.
(2) **Anne's and Henry's experiments** did not show the same results.

In Group D we are dealing with coordinate nouns in the possessive case.
Look at the two samples. In the first case Anne and Henry jointly possess
something. In the second, Anne and Henry separately possess something.
What is the difference in forming the possessive in each case?

● _____

  _____

  _____

Answer: When Anne and Henry possess something jointly, only *Henry* takes the possessive case. When they own something separately, both *Anne and Henry* take the possessive case.

In the phrases below fill in the blanks properly to form the possessive case.

Henry's   1. Anne and Henry____ signing of the will

Anne's and   2. Anne____ and Henry____ differing viewpoints
Henry's

In your own words, state the rule for forming the possessive for coordinate nouns:

● _____

_____

_____

Answer: When there is joint ownership, only the noun closest to the thing possessed takes the possessive case. When there is separate ownership, both nouns take the possessive case.

Group E: Possessive of indefinite pronouns.

(1) Who would win was **anyone's guess.**
(2) **Everybody's business** is **nobody's business.**

The pronouns in boldface type in Group E represent the class of pronouns known as indefinite pronouns. Look at them now. Other indefinite pronouns are **another, anything, either, everything, neither, no one, one, some, somebody, someone,** and **something.**

                           Do the examples in Group E seem to form the possessive
yes   in the usual way? _____

The rules you have already formulated for the words in the earlier groups apply to the indefinite pronouns.

In the sentences below fill in the blanks properly to form the possessive case:

either's   1. Has either____ coat been found?

somebody's   2. Somebody____ coat was found in the park.

One's   3. One____ identity should be protected.

Group F: Possessive of personal and relative pronouns.

(1) **Our car** is old but lovable.
(2) That **car of yours** is old and disgraceful.
(3) **Its missing left headlight** adds a raffish touch.
(4) **Whose car** it was, we have no idea.

The examples in boldface type demonstrate the possessive forms for the personal and relative pronouns: **my (mine), you (yours), his (his), her (hers), it (its), our (ours), their (theirs),** and **who (whose).** Examine the examples and the list just given. What significant departure from the rules for forming the possessive do you see?

● _____

_____

Answer: These pronouns form the possessive without the use of an apostrophe.

In the sentences below fill in the blanks properly to form the possessive case:

theirs   1. The picture was their____.

Whose   2. Who____ car was damaged?

mine, yours   3. My coat is mi____, and your coat is your____.

its*   4. That old house, it____ windows are broken.

Apostrophe for missing letters or numbers

Read each sentence below carefully. Examine closely portions that appear in boldface type.

(1) She **can't** run any faster.
(2) **It's** a good buy for the price.
(3) He was in Vietnam in **'72.**
(4) "We're **goin',**" he said, "don't rush us."

---

* The possessive form **its** is one of the most commonly misspelled words in English. Use **its** (without the apostrophe) whenever the possessive case is called for. Use **it's** (with the apostrophe) whenever you mean **it is.** There is no such word in English as **its'.**

1. **Can't** is a contraction, that is, a word formed by combining other words and omitting certain letters from them. What two words does **can't** replace?

can not   _____

contraction   2. **It's** is a con_____. What two words does

it is   it replace? _____

3. What mark of punctuation is used to replace the

apostrophe   missing letters in a contraction? _____

4. In **'72,** what number does the apostrophe replace?

19   ____

5. In **goin',** what letter does the apostrophe replace?

g   ____

In the following sentences fill in the blanks:

doesn't   1. Charlie doesn__t live here any longer.

It's   2. It__s only fair that she go.

o'clock   3. At 4 o__clock, school ends for the day.

'42   4. Most of the class of __42 faced World War II.

rushin', aroun' 5. "All this rushin__ aroun__! It's foolishness," he said.

In your own words state the rule for using the apostrophe for omitted letters or numbers:

● _____

_____

_____

Answer: Use an apostrophe to replace the missing letter(s) in contractions and to replace the missing letters or numbers in any word, phrase, or number set where letters or numbers are omitted.

Apostrophe for plural forms

Read each sentence below. Examine closely portions that appear in boldface type.

(1) The second grader made his **8's** and **9's** poorly.
(2) The third grader made his **a's** and **b's** very well.
(3) There were six **Ph.D.'s** at the party and two **M.D.'s**.
(4) The economy expanded in the early **1950s**.

In the first three examples, numbers, letters, and abbreviations are formed into the plural by adding an apostrophe plus an **s**. This is common practice to avoid the confusion of, for instance, mistaking **a's** for the word **as** or the plural **8's** for the expression **8s**.

However, notice in the last example that **1950s** is used without the apostrophe. Increasingly, when it can be done without confusing the reader, the apostrophe in these situations is omitted. In general, we would advise you to use the apostrophe with all single letters and numbers and with abbreviations that contain periods. When using longer numbers, numbers written as words, and abbreviations without periods, you can usually omit the apostrophe without fear of confusing the reader.

Fill in the blanks in the sentences below:

p's and q's   1. He knows his p____ and q____.

6's and 7's   2. They were at 6____ and 7____.

D.D.S.'s   3. The office had two D.D.S.____ in it.

DFCs   4. The crew received five DFC____ for bravery.

twos and threes   5. They came in two____ and three____.

1960s   6. The birthrate lowered in the early 1960____.

In your own words state the rules for using the apostrophe when forming the plurals of letters, numbers, and abbreviations:

- _____

_____

_____

_____

_____

Answer: Use an apostrophe and an s to form the plurals of single letters and numbers and of abbreviations that use periods. If you can do it without confusing the reader, use only an s when pluralizing longer numbers, numbers written as words, and abbreviations without periods.

PROOFREADING EXERCISE

(The passage below contains expressions that do not follow the rules you have learned in this chapter. Circle all such expressions; then write the expressions correctly in the numbered spaces provided. There may be more spaces provided than you need. Finally, check your answers with the key that follows.)

The Persian king Xerxes I conquered Athens in 480

B.C. However, in the same year he lost his fleet at

Salamis. Its' loss caused Xerxes to retreat to Asia. His

generals disappointment at the fleets loss was expressed

in the assassination of Xerxes. Trouble ran in two's for

Xerxes's family. His grandson Xerxes II was murdered

after a reign of only forty-five days. Thus, both Xerxes

I's and Xerxes II's reigns ended in murder. Its not

strange that neithers life was spared. Anyone who's

studies include this period knows that murder was a

tool of statecraft in those ancient times.

1. _____   2. _____   3. _____

4. _____   5. _____   6. _____

7. _____   8. _____   9. _____

Key: 1. *Its:* there is no such word as *its'* 2. *generals':* plural words ending in *s* take only the apostrophe in the possessive 3. *fleet's:* most singular words take an apostrophe and *s* in the possessive 4. *twos:* in general, numbers written as words do not use an apostrophe in the plural 5. *Xerxes':* words that end in an *eez* sound take only an apostrophe in the possessive 6. *It's* is the contraction of *it is* and, therefore, takes an apostrophe 7. *neither's:* indefinite pronouns take the apostrophe in the possessive 8. *whose:* relative pronouns do not take the apostrophe in the possessive

14 **The Demons**

Demons are the common words that tests show are more frequently misspelled than any others. For some you can find rules in this book to help you spell them correctly. When this is so we have listed the applicable chapter for you. For the others, either no rules exist, or what rules do exist are so complicated that other methods of fixing the correct spelling in your mind are actually easier.

Use any or all of the memorization devices that follow.

Pronunciation. Locate the demon in your dictionary. Using the dictionary's pronunciation key, be sure you pronounce the word correctly. (See Chapter 15.)

Writing, saying, hearing, and tracing. Carefully write the demon at least 10 times, saying the letters as you write them. When you complete the word pronounce it carefully. Listen to yourself as you write and speak. If you have access to a tape recorder, use it. Record your spelling of the word as you write and speak it. Then play the word back and trace over the letters of the written word as you hear them. With these methods you are fixing the word in your mind with both your aural and visual senses.

Mnemonic devices. Use mental association tricks to help you to remember the demon. Make up sentences that emphasize the troublesome part of the demon. Saying that it's c-c-cold in the **arCtic** will help you to remember to place the **c** in the word. Remembering that **MeN** march in a **coluMN** may help you visualize the **mn** that ends this word. The question, "**Is land** surrounded by water an **island**?" should help you with that demon. Mnemonic devices need not be logical or even sensible. The important thing is that they be memorable.

Here now is a list of demons. When possible a chapter has been noted.

angel	arouse	breathe
annual	article	brilliant
answer	attendance (6)	certain
around	auxiliary	column

conscientious	maneuver	psychology
dealt	many	recommend (10)
development (6)	meant	repetition (6)
embarrass (-ed) (6)	muscle	rhythm
etc.	necessary (6)	schedule
expense	nickel	separate (6)
familiar	obstacle	sergeant
fascinate	occasion (10)	shoulder
further	parallel	speech
guarantee (6)	pastime	stretch (ed)
guard	peculiar	syllable (6)
heroine	possess (es)	until
island	possession	vegetable
its (7, 13)	possible	vengeance
it's (7, 13)	prove	Wednesday
led (7)		

PROOFREADING EXERCISE

(Circle all misspelled words in the passage below; then write the words, cor rectly spelled, into the numbered spaces provided. There may be more spaces provided than words misspelled. Finally, check your answers with the key that follows.)

Its necesary to overcome all obstacles posible to guarantee

success. Guard against over-confidence. Remember — repetion

pays. By now you've dealt with many of your problems. Breath

a sigh of relief on this occassion. After all, you now know

you're a better speller.

1. _____ 2. _____ 3. _____

4. _____ 5. _____ 6. _____

Key: 1. it's 2. necessary 3. possible 4. repetition 5. breathe 6. occasion

112

15 Using Your Dictionary

For the times when our rules can't solve a spelling problem for you or when you want the comfort of another source to confirm that you have applied a rule correctly, you will need a dictionary.

Dictionaries, which came into being during the seventeenth and eighteenth centuries, have standardized our spelling. Even though pronunciation has changed over time and in different English speaking countries, the spelling has remained essentially the same.* At first glance this may seem unreasonable and arbitrary. As we have seen in several chapters, most notably Chapter 6, "Unstressed Vowels," pronunciation shifts can, indeed, cause spelling problems. But, think for a moment. What would be the result if spelling were based exclusively on pronunciation? Whose pronunciation would we use? Oxford English, Canadian English, Midwestern American English, Mississippi English, or Australian English? If, as is likely, each country or region chose its spelling to match its own pronunciation, the different spellings would soon fragment English into many separate languages. As users of a worldwide, increasingly universal language, we English speakers, despite some inconveniences, are probably fortunate that English spelling has been frozen in place.

In any case, dictionaries are where we go to confirm the spelling of our language. To be a good speller, you have to know how to use these valuable books. To begin with, buy a reputable dictionary. Don't buy marked-down remainders or bargain dictionaries. For most people, any of the college level dictionaries, such as *The American Heritage Dictionary of the English Language,* from which we draw our examples, will serve well. If in doubt, check with a reliable bookseller.

Read the introduction to your dictionary and browse through its contents. Learn the ways you can use the dictionary to aid your spelling. For now,

---

* With only very minor differences, such as American English **harbor** and **center** vs. British **harbour** and **centre.**

look at the entry below and we'll point out some of the information you can glean from it.

con·ceive (kən-sēv') *v.* -ceived, -ceiving, -ceives. —*tr.* **1.** To become pregnant with. **2.** To form in the mind; imagine. **3.** To apprehend mentally; understand. **4.** To express in particular words. **5.** To think or believe; hold an opinion. —*intr.* **1.** To form an idea. Used with *of.* **2.** To become pregnant. [Middle English *conceiven,* from Old French *conceivre,* from Latin *concipere,* to take to oneself, hence to be impregnated, to take into the mind : *com-,* comprehensively + *capere,* to take (see **kap-** in Appendix*).] —**con·ceiv'a·bil'i·ty,** **con·ceiv'a·ble·ness** *n.* —**con·ceiv'a·ble** *adj.* —**con·ceiv'a·bly** *adv.* —**con·ceiv'er** *n.*

Copyright © 1982 Houghton Mifflin Company. Reprinted by permission from *The American Heritage Dictionary of the English Language,* 2nd college edition.

Note the entry word itself, **conceive.** It has been broken into syllables with a dot between syllables — information you need when you have to hyphenate a word at the end of a line. Be careful to distinguish between the dots used to indicate syllabication and the hyphens used in such hyphenated words as **self-rule.**

The phonetic spelling following the entry word gives you the correct pronunciation, often important in spelling as you have seen in Chapter 5, "Pronunciation Difficulties." (A key to the pronunciation symbols used will appear at the bottom of every page in a reputable dictionary.) Note the accent mark on the second syllable, showing you where the word is accented — valuable information when you are applying the fourfold final consonant rule explained in Chapter 3.

Following the pronunciation is a small **v** indicating the word is a verb. This is followed by the endings for the principal parts of the verb: **-ceived, -ceiving,** and **-ceives.** Now you have four spellings: **conceive, conceived, conceiving,** and **conceives.**

At the end of the entry the dictionary will usually list related words formed by adding various suffixes to the entry word, in this case, the five words **conceivability, conceivableness, conceivable, conceivably,** and **conceiver.**

From this one entry alone, you have nine words with their correct spellings.

Entries for nouns will give the plurals for nouns when they are irregular or, as is the case of words that end in **o,** present difficulties. The dictionary, therefore, will tell us that the plural for **medium** is **media,** except in the case of a **medium** communicating with the dead, in which case the plural is **mediums.** From the dictionary we learn that the plural for **silo** is **silos,** but the plural for **potato** is **potatoes.**

Entries for adjectives will give the spellings for all degrees of adjectives, as in **moist, moister,** and **moistest,** and for the adverbs and nouns formed from adjectives, as in **moistly** and **moistness.**

When there is a variant spelling for a word, the variant will follow the entry word. When it immediately follows the entry word, as in "**ax, axe,**" neither spelling is preferred over the other. When the variant is introduced with an **also,** as in "**judgment.** . . . Also **judgement,**" the entry word is the preferred spelling. When the variant is British or regional, the dictionary specifies, as in "**labor.** . . . Also chiefly British **labour.**" In this case, when preparing documents for use in the United States, choose the entry word spelling of **labor.**

As a review, read over the following dictionary entry and answer the questions that follow it. The answers appear at the bottom of the page.

> **de·fense** (di-fĕns′) *n.* Also *chiefly British* **de·fence.** *Abbr.* **def.**
> **1.** The act of defending against attack, danger, or injury; protection. **2.** Anything that defends or protects. **3.** *Psychoanalysis.* An unconsciously acquired, involuntarily operating mental attribute, mechanism, or dynamism, such as regression, repression, reaction-formation, or projection, that protects the individual from shame, anxiety, or loss of self-esteem. **4.** An argument in support or justification of something. **5.** *Law.* **a.** The action of the defendant in opposition to complaints against him. **b.** The defendant and his legal counsel. **6.** The science or art of defending oneself; self-defense. **7.** *Sports.* The team or those players on the team attempting to stop the opposition from scoring. —*tr.v.* **defensed, -fensing, -fenses.** *Football.* To act as defense: *defense a play.* [Middle English *defens(e),* from Old French, from Latin *dēfensa,* from the feminine past participle of *dēfendere,* DEFEND.] —**de·fense′less** *adj.* —**de·fense′less·ly** *adv.* —**de·fense′less·ness** *n.*
>
> Copyright © 1982 Houghton Mifflin Company. Reprinted by permission from *The American Heritage Dictionary of the English Language,* 2nd college edition.

(1) How many syllables in the word **defense**?
(2) On which syllable does the accent fall?
(3) What is the variant spelling?
(4) In the United States which is the preferred spelling?
(5) What are the principal parts of the verb **defense**?
(6) What are the adjective and adverb derived from **defense**?

Answers: 1. two 2. second 3. defence 4. defense 5. defensed, defensing, defenses 6. defenseless, defenselessly

Progress Check

This is your opportunity to see exactly how much improvement you have made with your spelling. To insure meaningful comparisons you'll find the same type of test items that were used initially to diagnose your problems. Compare your initial scores with scores on the test which follows. Then savor the satisfaction of seeing definite measurable evidence of your growth and achievement. Now — go right ahead with the progress test.

SPELLING PROGRESS CHECK

Each of the following sentences contains a potential spelling problem, including problems with hyphens and apostrophes. Spell each word in question in the space to the right of the sentence. Blank spaces call attention to trouble spots. Add any needed letter, letters, hyphens, or apostrophes to complete the spelling. With some, no letters or marks need be added to spell the word correctly.

Pay no attention to the numbers at the end of each line. They will be explained later.

1. Try hop____g on your other foot. _____ (4)

2. He's our (quarter back / quarter-back / quarterback). _____ (12)

3. You can't fail — you're sure to suc_____. _____ (7)

4. Take your gr__vance to the boss. _____ (1)

5. The money benefit__ed them greatly. _____ (3)

6. They are writ__g a new set of rules. _____ (9)

7. Of the three cats, which is the livel__st? _____ (2)

8. There__s no reason to leave now. _____ (13)

9. Both attorn__s were in the office. _____ (11)

10. A passport is nec____sary for France. _____ (14)

11. This room will a__commodate your students. _____ (10)

116

12. I looked at them cool__y before leaving. _____ (8)

13. Follow the same proced____ next time. _____ (6)

14. The unexpected call was a su__prise. _____ (5)

15. Will you carry my br__fcase? _____ (1)

16. That meal is served in the din__g room. _____ (4)

17. What advi__e can you give me? _____ (7)

18. Are you di__satisfied with the results? _____ (8)

19. Who is judg__g the next case? _____ (9)

20. Ship this box by fr__ght. _____ (1)

21. Put the sheets into sep__rate files. _____ (6)

22. My car has four__wheel brakes. _____ (12)

23. You must measure the wind__s velocity. _____ (13)

24. Several wires had come lo__se. _____ (14)

25. I accident__ly fell downstairs. _____ (5)

26. Are you still stud____g economics? _____ (2)

27. I ate two tomato__s for lunch. _____ (11)

28. Be sure to start at the begin____g. _____ (3)

29. Our mail carr__r is new on the route. _____ (2)

30. This letter is almost i__legible. _____ (10)

31. Buy two loa__s of bread for supper. _____ (11)

32. When did you rec__ve the package? _____ (1)

33. Ath__tics is over-emphasized here. _____ (5)

34. How many box__s came in the mail? _____ (11)

35. The incident occur__d yesterday. _____ (3)

36. What a capit__l idea! _____ (7)

37. Which route do you re__commend? _____ (10)

38. These notes are all up__to__date. _____ (12)

39. Par__lel lines meet at infinity. _____ (14)

40. The student was bus__ly at work. _____ (2)

41. Try grip____g the club at the end. _____ (4)

42. Have you ever taken a sp__ch course? _____ (14)

43. The student___s friend visited class. _____ (13)

44. I was real___y tired after the race. _____ (8)

45. They arg___d about it all evening. _____ (9)

46. Are you quit___g early again today? _____ (3)

47. I'll meet you in the lib___ry later. _____ (5)

48. Which act___r played the lead in the play? _____ (6)

49. How many words did you mis___pell? _____ (8)

50. Twenty___three students were present. _____ (12)

51. Charles___ coat seems to need cleaning. _____ (13)

52. That's the nicest compl___ment ever. _____ (7)

53. Why not get an independ___nt opinion? _____ (6)

54. A monkey was shin_____g up a flagpole. _____ (4)

55. Some are more chang___able than others. _____ (9)

56. They waited for my a___pearance. _____ (10)

Check your answers carefully, using the answer key on page 120. Circle the words you misspelled, including the figure in parentheses immediately after the spelling.

When you have checked all 56 items, tally your results in the appropriate boxes below, just as you did with the diagnostic test. The boxes are numbered to correspond to the identifying numbers following each blank in the test. For each misspelling, note the identifying number after the blank and place a tally mark in the correspondingly numbered box below, as in the sample.

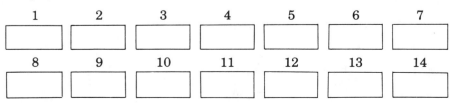

Sample

12

The sample indicates that only one item in area 12 was missed. As you remember, the area numbers correspond to the chapter numbers in this book.

Tally of Problem Areas

1	2	3	4	5	6	7

8	9	10	11	12	13	14

When you have completed your tally of errors, compare your scores with the initial tally on page 8. You can then see exactly how much improvement you have made. Of course, in this 56-item progress check, each of the four-teen areas is covered by exactly four words, not ten as in the diagnostic test — a shorter coverage. To insure accurate comparisons, however, the first fourteen items on this progress check came directly from the initial diag-nostic check, one from each of the fourteen areas. Notice whether or not you missed any of the first fourteen items. If you did, look back at the diagnostic test to see how many you missed initially — an exact indication of im-provement. Suppose you missed six of those fourteen items initially (60%) and only one in this mini-check (25%). Reducing errors from 60 percent to 25 percent is progress indeed.

Now try another proofreading check for evidence of improvement in that area.

PROOFREADING CHECK

In the following passage underline all the spelling errors, including any in-volving a hyphen or apostrophe. Use the same care you would normally take in correcting your own work.

1 When you complete this check, look back on you're proofreading

2 score from the begining diagnostic test. We're hopping you'll

3 then see exactly how much improvement studyng this book has

4 brought. It's not to soon for you to perceive certian gains.

5 Mispellings should definitely be easier to spot in your writting in

6 all fourteen categorys covered. If you've been persistant in your

7 efforts and if you've given attention to apropriate, well chosen

8 problem areas, disasterous spelling errors should indeed be

9 minimized. We do not decieve you. Comparison of this score with

10 your earlier proofreading score will make the point clear.

Check your answers with the key on page 120.

Answers to Progress Check

1. hopping	20. freight	39. Parallel
2. quarterback	21. separate	40. busily
3. succeed	22. four-wheel	41. gripping
4. grievance	23. wind's	42. speech
5. benefited	24. loose	43. student's
6. writing	25. accidentally	44. really
7. liveliest	26. studying	45. argued
8. There's	27. tomatoes	46. quitting
9. attorneys	28. beginning	47. library
10. necessary	29. carrier	48. actor
11. accommodate	30. illegible	49. misspell
12. coolly	31. loaves	50. Twenty-three
13. procedure	32. receive	51. Charles'
14. surprise	33. Athletics	52. compliment
15. briefcase	34. boxes	53. independent
16. dining	35. occurred	54. shinning
17. advice	36. capital	55. changeable
18. dissatisfied	37. recommend	56. appearance
19. judging	38. up-to-date	

Answers to Proofreading Check

You should have underlined the following 14 words and only those words. The correct form is provided below. In this part of the test, one word from each of the 14 problem areas was introduced. Count as an error any misspelled word not underlined and any correctly spelled word underlined. To make your proofreading score exactly comparable, the identical words used in the diagnostic test were repeated here, except in different context.

Spelling used	*Correct spelling*	*Problem area*	*Percent missing word*
you're (line 1)	your	13	27%
begining (line 2)	beginning	3	29%
hopping (line 2)	hoping	4	39%
studyng (line 3)	studying	2	12%
to (line 4)	too	7	58%
certian (line 4)	certain	14	25%
mispellings (line 5)	misspellings	8	34%
writting (line 5)	writing	9	20%
categorys (line 6)	categories	11	17%
persistant (line 6)	persistent	6	71%
apropriate (line 7)	appropriate	10	8%
well chosen (line 7)	well-chosen	12	90%
disasterous (line 8)	disastrous	5	61%
decieve (line 9)	deceive	1	31%

If you underlined words other than the 14 listed on page 120, enter them in correctly spelled form on pages 132–133, with other personal spelling problems.

For an exact comparison, use the table below to get a percentile rank. Then compare your rank on this progress check with that on your diagnostic proofreading test to see how much improvement you have made. (See page 12.)

Number of errors	Percentile rank
0	100
1	97
2	89
3	75
4	56
5	40
6	29
7	23
8	12
9	6
10	3

Now look back at your tally of results on the spelling part of the progress check. Let those results guide you to make last-minute adjustments to bring an even stronger feeling of mastery. For example, suppose you now have some areas with absolutely no tallied errors. Congratulate yourself on achieving such a mastery of those problem areas. Suppose a further look shows you several areas where you tallied only one error. That suggests you are right on the verge of mastery. Take a minute to look at the word misspelled and back at the chapter involved. Refresh yourself on that particular aspect of the problem and quickly eliminate the last remaining difficulty. If there are areas where you tallied two errors, you need to make a more extensive review — time well spent. Finally, if there are still areas where you missed three or four of the four items, you have major handicaps remaining. This means careful, thorough review of the chapter in question, with special attention to the specific words that are still giving you trouble. Once those moves are made, however, you will see that your efforts have paid off handsomely.

A Final Word

We have tried in this little book to simplify and digest the rules that committed to memory will make spelling easier for you — easier but not easy, unfortunately. No easy, high road to spelling perfection really exists. For many historical reasons, some of which we have told you about, English is one of the most difficult of all languages in its spelling. Yet, we have also attempted to show you that the situation is not totally hopeless, if you care enough about your spelling to put some effort into it.

It is really not enough for you to have worked your way through this book to this point. You must now conscientiously apply the rules you have learned whenever you write. Only through constant application will the rules become part of your habit patterns to the point where they become second nature to you. If you revert to guessing at the spelling of words, or even using the dictionary in cases where the rules would guide you to the correct spelling of a word, you will soon forget all you have learned. Don't, for example, resort to the dictionary for the correct spelling of the plural of **activity.** Remember, instead, that all words that end in a consonant plus **y** are pluralized by changing the final **y** to **i** and adding **es,** thus **activities.** Remember the rules that do work and apply them. In so doing you will save yourself valuable time and grow confident in the application of the rules.

Keep this little book handy to your desk. When you forget a rule, as we all do, find the correct chapter and check the rule. Work through the sequence again if necessary. In time you will know the spelling rules as well as you know other complicated mental sequences. Multiplication tables, street addresses, telephone numbers, song lyrics — none of these are really easy to memorize. You have learned them through constant repetition. Put the same principle to work in your spelling.

How about the words that do not lend themselves to spelling by the rules — words with unstressed vowels, for example, or the sound-alike words like **principle** and **principal?** For such words apply the four-track method of writing, saying, hearing, and tracing that we told you about in Chapter 14. Write the word, say the word correctly, and listen as you do. Read the word, trace it over, saying it as you do. Use it in sentences that demonstrate that you know its correct meaning. Make your own mnemonic devices for some words as we did in Chapters 6 and 14. Use your dictionary for words that are difficult to spell and that you don't use often enough to make memorizing them worthwhile. Neither of your authors would dream of spelling **reconnaissance** without looking it up in the dictionary.

The road to good spelling is not easy, but it is not an impossible road. If good spelling is important to you, you can reach your goal.

PROOFREADING EXERCISE

Words representing Chapters 1–14 are in this exercise. Some of them are misspelled. Circle the misspelled words; then write them correctly below into the numbered spaces provided. There may be more spaces provided than words misspelled. Finally, check your answers with the key that follows.)

Undoubtedly, humankinds greatest achievement was the
invention of language. Because when language first made its
apearance it was spoken and not written, in all likelyhood we'll
never know how it first came into being. But think of the
obstacles between human beings, the intellectual loneliness we
would live in, without language. Because we have this unusual
gift, we can communicate across the barriers of time and space.
Through language we can engage in selfexpression, arguement,
and business. If language had not occured, our enviroment would
be very different. All oportunities for progress would have been
stopped at some primitive stage of our existence. We would seem
closer to monkies than what we have become. Truly, in the
beginning was the word.

1. _____   2. _____   3. _____

4. _____   5. _____   6. _____

7. _____   8. _____   9. _____

Key: If you miss a word, review the chapter indicated. 1. *humankind's*, Ch. 13. 2. *appearance*, Ch. 6. 3. *likelihood*, Ch. 2. 4. *self-expression*, Ch. 12. 5. *arguement*, Ch. 9. 6. *occurred*, Ch. 3. 7. *environment*, Ch. 5. 8. *opportunities*, Ch. 10. 9. *monkeys*, Ch. 11.

Appendix

CORE WORDS

	*	**		*	**
1. absence	6	6	32. arouse(d)	4	14
2. absorption	3	5, 8	33. arrangement(s)	4	9
3. accidentally	6	5	34. article	3	14
4. accommodate(s)	7	10	35. ascend	3	5
5. accomplish	3	8	36. athlete	3	5
6. achievement	3	1	37. athletic	4	5
7. acquire	3	5	38. author	3	6
8. across	6	10	39. auxiliary	3	14
9. advise	4	7	40. beginning	5	3
10. affect	3	7	41. believe(d)	6	1
11. against	3	8	42. benefit	5	6
12. all right	7	7	43. benefited	6	3
13. almost	6	7	44. breathe	4	14
14. already	6	7	45. brilliant	3	14
15. although	3	7	46. business	6	2
16. altogether	4	7	47. calendar	3	6
17. amateur	5	6	48. careful	3	9
18. among	5	10	49. carrying	4	2
19. analysis	4	6	50. ceiling	3	1
20. analyze	5	5	51. cemetery	4	6
21. angel	3	14	52. certain	6	14
22. annual	3	14	53. changeable	5	9
23. answer	3	14	54. chief	3	1
24. apparatus	3	10	55. choose	5	5
25. apparent	6	6, 10	56. chose(n)	6	9
26. appearance	5	6	57. clothes	4	7
27. appropriate	5	10	58. column	3	14
28. Arctic	4	5	59. coming	6	9, 10
29. arguing	4	9	60. committed	3	3, 10
30. argument	7	9	61. committee	6	3, 10
31. around	4	14	62. comparatively	3	6, 8

* Number of lists of problem words that this word appears on.
** Chapters where principles governing this word are discussed.

125

63.	conceive	5	1	112. except	4	7
64.	conceivable	3	9	113. exercise	3	6
65.	conscience	4	1	114. existence	8	6
66.	conscientious	5	1, 14	115. expense	4	14
67.	conscious	6	7	116. experience	5	6
68.	consistent	4	3, 6	117. experiment	3	6
69.	continuous	3	5	118. explanation	3	6
70.	control	4	6	119. extremely	3	8
71.	controlled	5	3, 6	120. familiar	6	14
72.	convenience	4	5	121. fascinate	6	14
73.	counsel	3	7	122. February	5	5
74.	criticism	3	5	123. finally	6	8
75.	criticize	4	5	124. financier	3	1
76.	curiosity	3	6	125. foreign	5	1
77.	cylinder	3	6	126. foresee	3	7
78.	dealt	3	14	127. forty	7	7
79.	decide(d)	3	6	128. fourth	4	7
80.	decision	4	6	129. friend	5	1
81.	definite(ly)	8	6, 9	130. fundamental	5	6
82.	description	3	6	131. further	3	14
83.	desirable	3	6, 9	132. generally	5	8
84.	despair	6	6	133. government	6	5
85.	destroy	3	6	134. governor	4	5, 6
86.	develop	5	6	135. grammar	7	6
87.	development	3	6, 14	136. grateful	3	7
88.	difference	3	6	137. guarantee	3	6, 14
89.	different	3	5, 10	138. guard	4	14
90.	dining	4	4	139. guidance	3	6
91.	disappear(ed)	6	8	140. height	3	1, 5
92.	disappoint	4	6, 10	141. heroes	5	11
93.	disastrous	5	5	142. heroine	3	14
94.	discipline	4	6	143. hoping	3	4
95.	disease(s)	5	6	144. humorous	4	3
96.	dissatisfied	3	8, 10	145. imaginary	3	9
97.	distinction	3	6	146. imagination	4	6
98.	divide(d)	5	6	147. immediately	6	9
99.	divine	6	6	148. incidentally	6	5, 8
100.	easily	3	2	149. independence	4	6
101.	effect	7	7	150. independent	4	6
102.	efficient	3	6	151. indispensable	5	6
103.	eligible	3	6	152. influential	4	6
104.	embarrass(ed & ment)	7	6, 14	153. intellectual	3	6
105.	enemy	3	6	154. intelligence	5	6
106.	environment	5	5	155. intelligent	3	6
107.	equipped	6	3	156. interest(ed)	5	6
108.	especially	4	8	157. interfere	3	4
109.	etc.	3	14	158. irrelevant	6	5, 10
110.	exaggerate(d)	4	6, 9	159. island	3	14
111.	excellent	5	3, 6	160. it's	5	7, 13

161. its	6	7, 13	
162. jealous	3	6	
163. judgment	7	9	
164. kindergarten	3	7	
165. knowledge	7	6	
166. laboratory	5	5	
167. laid	5	7	
168. larynx	3	5	
169. later	4	4	
170. led	6	7, 14	
171. leisure	4	1	
172. length	3	5	
173. library	4	5, 6	
174. license	4	6	
175. likelihood	3	2	
176. likely	3	8	
177. livelihood	3	2	
178. loneliness	5	2	
179. lose	7	7	
180. magazine	4	6	
181. maintenance	5	6	
182. maneuver	3	14	
183. many	3	14	
184. marriage	6	6	
185. mathematics	5	5	
186. meant	6	14	
187. medicine	4	6	
188. miniature	5	5	
189. morale	4	7	
190. muscle	3	14	
191. naturally	4	8	
192. necessary	7	6, 14	
193. neighbor	3	1, 6	
194. neither	3	1	
195. nickel	4	14	
196. niece	4	1	
197. ninety	6	9	
198. ninth	5	9	
199. noticeable	8	9	
200. obstacle	3	14	
201. occasion	5	10, 14	
202. occasionally	3	8, 10	
203. occur	3	3, 10	
204. occurred	7	3	
205. occurrence	6	3, 6	
206. official	3	6	
207. omit	4	10	
208. omitted	4	3	
209. opinion	5	6	
210. opportunity	4	10	
211. optimism	4	6	
212. origin	3	6	
213. original	4	6, 10	
214. paid	4	7	
215. parallel	7	14	
216. particularly	4	8	
217. pastime	4	14	
218. peaceable	3	9	
219. peculiar	3	14	
220. perceive	3	1	
221. perform	4	5	
222. permanent	3	6	
223. personal	3	6	
224. perspiration	3	5	
225. persuade	3	14	
226. pertain	3	6	
227. piece	3	1	
228. planned	3	3	
229. playwright	3	7	
230. pleasant	4	6	
231. poison	3	6	
232. politician	3	6	
233. possess(es)	5	14	
234. possession	3	14	
235. possible	3	14	
236. practical	4	9	
237. precede	7	5, 7	
238. prefer	3	5	
239. preferred	3	3, 5	
240. prejudice(d)	5	6	
241. preparation	3	5, 6	
242. prepare	4	5	
243. prevalent	4	6	
244. primitive	4	6	
245. principal	3	7	
246. principle	3	7	
247. privilege	7	6	
248. probably	4	5, 8	
249. procedure	6	6	
250. proceed	7	7	
251. professor	6	6, 8, 10	
252. prove	4	14	
253. psychology	3	14	
254. pursue	5	6	
255. pursuit	4	6	
256. quantity	6	5	
257. quiet	3	6	
258. realize	3	5	

127

259.	receipt	3	1	298.	symmetrical	3	6, 10
260.	receive	8	1	299.	temperament	3	5
261.	recognize	3	5	300.	temperature	3	5
262.	recommend	6	10, 14	301.	tendency	3	6
263.	regard	3	6	302.	than	4	7
264.	relieve	4	1, 6	303.	their	6	1, 7
265.	religious	3	6	304.	then	3	7
266.	repetition	6	6, 14	305.	there	5	7
267.	resistance	3	6	306.	therefore	3	7
268.	rhythm	4	14	307.	they're	3	7
269.	ridiculous	4	6	308.	thorough	4	7
270.	safety	5	9	309.	thought	3	7
271.	scene	4	7	310.	through	3	7
272.	schedule	6	14	311.	together	5	6
273.	science	3	1	312.	too	5	7
274.	seize	6	1	313.	tragedy	4	5
275.	sense	4	7	314.	tries	4	2
276.	separate	9	6, 14	315.	truly	6	9
277.	sergeant	5	14	316.	undoubtedly	3	8
278.	several	3	6	317.	until	7	14
279.	shepherd	4	6	318.	unusual	3	8
280.	shining	6	4	319.	using	3	9
281.	shoulder	3	14	320.	usually	4	8
282.	significant	3	6	321.	vacuum	4	6
283.	similar	7	6	322.	vegetable	4	14
284.	simile	3	6	323.	vengeance	3	14
285.	sophomore	4	5	324.	villain	6	6
286.	specimen	4	6	325.	weather	5	7
287.	speech	5	14	326.	Wednesday	4	14
288.	stopped	3	4	327.	weird	7	1
289.	straight	3	7	328.	where	3	7
290.	strength	5	5	329.	whether	6	7
291.	strenuous	3	6	330.	wholly	3	7, 8
292.	stretch(ed)	5	14	331.	whose	6	7
293.	studying	6	2	332.	woman	4	6
294.	succeed	6	7	333.	women	3	6
295.	suppress	3	10	334.	writing	6	9
296.	surprise(s)	6	5	335.	written	3	4
297.	syllable	3	6, 14	336.	you're	5	7

1. accessible
2. accompanied
3. accustomed
4. achieve
5. address
6. advice
7. adviser
8. aerial
9. aisle
10. always
11. amount
12. an
13. anoint
14. antiseptic
15. appear
16. appetite
17. approaching
18. aroused
19. arrangements
20. assistant
21. awful
22. balloon
23. basically
24. before
25. believed
26. buried
27. busy
28. cafeteria
29. calculate
30. capital
31. captain
32. category
33. cede
34. changing
35. characteristic
36. chosen
37. climbed
38. common
39. comparative
40. competition
41. compliment
42. concentration
43. concern
44. connoisseur
45. conquer
46. consider
47. continually
48. conversation
49. coolly
50. copies
51. corroborate
52. councilor
53. countries
54. course
55. courteous
56. crowd
57. crystal
58. deceive
59. decided
60. definitely
61. definition
62. degree
63. dependent
64. derelict
65. describe
66. desperate
67. dessert
68. determine
69. device
70. didn't
71. dilemma
72. dilettante
73. disappeared
74. disappointed
75. disapprove
76. discoveries
77. discriminate
78. discussed
79. dissection
80. dissipate
81. dissipation
82. divided
83. division
84. doesn't
85. dormitories
86. drunkenness
87. ecstasy
88. efficiency
89. eighth
90. eliminated
91. embarrassed
92. embarrassment
93. emphasize
94. engines
95. equipment
96. essential
97. exaggerated
98. exceed
99. exhausted
100. exhilaration
101. fascinating
102. financial
103. flourish
104. forcibly
105. formerly
106. forth
107. forward
108. freshman
109. frightening
110. gardener
111. grievous
112. hadn't
113. handle
114. here
115. holiday
116. hungry
117. hurriedly
118. hurrying
119. identity
120. imbecile
121. imitation
122. immigrant
123. increase
124. inevitably
125. initiate
126. inoculate
127. insistent
128. interested
129. interpreted
130. invitation
131. irresistible
132. irritable
133. knew
134. lightning
135. literally
136. literature
137. losing
138. loyalty

139. lying
140. married
141. merely
142. minutes
143. mischievous
144. misspelled
145. misspelling
146. mournful
147. mysterious
148. Negroes
149. nevertheless
150. newsstand
151. o'clock
152. operate
153. optimist
154. optimistic
155. oscillate
156. panicky
157. particular
158. partner
159. perhaps
160. persistent
161. perseverance
162. personally
163. plain
164. planning
165. plebeian
166. populace
167. porch
168. portrayed
169. possesses
170. practically
171. prairie
172. preceding
173. predictable
174. preference
175. prejudiced
176. preparations
177. presence
178. principles
179. proceeded
180. professional
181. prominent
182. pronunciation
183. propeller
184. prophecy
185. prophesied
186. proved
187. quarter
188. really
189. recede
190. received
191. referred
192. representative
193. resemblance
194. respectability
195. restaurant
196. rhythmical
197. roommate
198. sacrifice
199. sacrilegious
200. scarcely
201. secretary
202. sentence
203. severely
204. sheriff
205. signal
206. sincerely
207. sleeve
208. source
209. speak
210. statement
211. stationary
212. stationery
213. stretched
214. striking
215. successful
216. suddenness
217. superintendent
218. supersede
219. surely
220. tariff
221. title
222. to
223. toward
224. tranquillity
225. transferred
226. twelfth
227. tyrannize
228. university
229. unnecessary
230. vacillate
231. versatile
232. vicious
233. village
234. whereabouts
235. won't

As a useful addendum for you, we include the new Postal Service abbreviations for states and a list of common metric terms and their abbreviations. The first is now needed for correct correspondence, and the second becomes increasingly useful as the United States moves toward the adoption of the metric system.

Postal Service State Abbreviations

Alabama	AL	Montana	MT
Alaska	AK	Nebraska	NE
Arizona	AZ	Nevada	NV
Arkansas	AR	New Hampshire	NH
California	CA	New Jersey	NJ
Colorado	CO	New Mexico	NM
Connecticut	CT	New York	NY
Delaware	DE	North Carolina	NC
District of Columbia	DC	North Dakota	ND
Florida	FL	Ohio	OH
Georgia	GA	Oklahoma	OK
Guam	GU	Oregon	OR
Hawaii	HI	Pennsylvania	PA
Idaho	ID	Puerto Rico	PR
Illinois	IL	Rhode Island	RI
Indiana	IN	South Carolina	SC
Iowa	IA	South Dakota	SD
Kansas	KS	Tennessee	TN
Kentucky	KY	Texas	TX
Louisiana	LA	Utah	UT
Maine	ME	Vermont	VT
Maryland	MD	Virginia	VA
Massachusetts	MA	Virgin Islands	VI
Michigan	MI	Washington	WA
Minnesota	MN	West Virginia	WV
Mississippi	MS	Wisconsin	WI
Missouri	MO	Wyoming	WY

Common Metric Terms and Their Abbreviations

millimeter	mm	milligram	mg	milliliter	ml
centimeter	cm	centigram	cg	centiliter	cl
decimeter	dm	decigram	dg	deciliter	dl
meter	m	gram	g	liter	L
dekameter	dam	dekagram	dag	dekaliter	dal
hectometer	hm	hectogram	hg	hectoliter	hl
kilometer	km	kilogram	kg	kiloliter	kl

The very book that provides *you* with maximum spelling help is, in all probability, not the one to provide equal help to another. Your own spelling problems are, in a sense, like your own fingerprints. They are to a degree distinctively your own — not anyone else's. That means that this book, if it is to be most useful, should fit your needs, exactly, not someone else's.

These pages should do exactly that — fit the book most closely to your very own needs. As you work through the book, whenever you misspell a word, enter it below. These are words you *know* give you trouble. They are words you've actually misspelled.

Review the list periodically. Use mnemonic devices, an appropriate rule, or the four-step approach to fix the correct spelling indelibly in mind.

A_____   D_____   G_____

_____   _____   _____

_____   _____   _____

_____   _____   _____

B_____   E_____   H_____

_____   _____   _____

_____   _____   _____

_____   _____   _____

C_____   F_____   I_____

_____   _____   _____

_____   _____   _____

_____   _____   _____

_____   _____   _____

J_____

_____

_____

_____

_____

K_____

_____

_____

_____

_____

L_____

_____

_____

_____

_____

M_____

_____

_____

_____

_____

N_____

_____

_____

_____

_____

O_____

_____

_____

_____

_____

P_____

_____

_____

_____

_____

Q_____

_____

_____

_____

_____

R_____

_____

_____

_____

_____

S_____

_____

_____

_____

_____

T_____

_____

_____

_____

_____

U_____

_____

_____

_____

_____

V_____

_____

_____

_____

_____

W_____

_____

_____

_____

_____

X_____

_____

_____

_____

_____

Y_____

_____

_____

_____

_____

Z_____

_____

_____

_____

_____